THE FITNESS ENTREPRENEUR'S HANDBOOK

by

PAT RIGSBY

Table of Contents

Foreward

As an aspiring strength and conditioning coach, it quickly became readily apparent to me that book smarts would only take me so far in the fitness industry. You see, being a successful fitness professional is equal parts *science and art*.

You can learn plenty of physiology, kinesiology, and biomechanics principles from textbooks, college courses, seminars, and DVDs – and you can usually do it pretty rapidly, if you're willing to hustle and put in the work. When it comes to the art portion of the success equation, though, it takes a lot of patience because it can't be rushed.

Since every client is unique, you realize that the art is in finding the right mix for each individual. Does an athlete in front of you respond to kinesthetic, auditory, or verbal cues? Is he an introvert or extrovert? Does she have pre-existing misconceptions about what training entails? Is there an injury history around which you have to work? Are you dealing with a limited equipment scenario? Does your client only have two hours per week to devote to exercise? The list could go on and on, but the lesson doesn't change: you need to see a ton of clients over many years to become a successful "artist" who can put all the pieces together to deliver successful outcomes.

Perhaps not surprisingly, there are some interesting parallels on the business side of the fitness industry. You can't just read business books and expect to understand how to run a profitable gym. And, my own business partner often jokes that his MBA education really does very little to help him in running our facility. The only way to truly learn how to run a successful fitness business is to run one – and interact with loads of other fitness business owners to see what's worked and what hasn't.

Pat Rigsby has built this "sample size" as well as anyone I've encountered in my time in the fitness industry.

Pat has run multiple successful businesses both in the in-person and online realms. He's consulted for loads of successful businesses, including Cressey Sports Performance. In fact, I often joke that Pat is probably the best listener in the fitness industry for putting up with all my questions and hearing out all my ideas. Truth be told, though, he's listened to (and coached) folks from all corners of the industry, and that's why you'll find him to be such a versatile business coach in the pages that follow.

This is a book that's rooted in experience, trial and error, and a genuine passion for adding (not extracting) value for your customers. Let Pat help show you the way to building your ideal business – and faster than you thought possible.

Eric Cressey
President, Cressey Sports Performance
www.EricCressey.com

Introduction

During my time in the fitness industry, I have watched many people aspire to success. I am one of those people, and while I'm certainly a work in progress, I have had my fair share of success already and also have helped thousands of fitness entrepreneurs just like you achieve great successes of their own.

Because of this I'm often asked what my "secrets" to success are. I don't think they're secrets, but every one of us needs to have a formula that works on a personal level. This book is a collection of essays that share the strategies, tactics, and the mindset 'secrets' that have led me and the fitness entrepreneurs I have worked with to the successes that we've collectively achieved and that will undoubtedly be the foundation for our future successes.

Here are my suggestions on how to use this book:

I've written each chapter so that it can stand on its own as a lesson that you can take immediate action on, so don't feel that you have to read the entire book before you can start deriving benefit from it. Read a chapter, and apply what you've learned. Take action.

If you approach the book in this fashion, I can guarantee that you will benefit greatly from this resource. The lessons in *The Fitness Entrepreneur's Handbook* have helped trainers and coaches open their own facilities, grow six and seven figure a year businesses, enjoy more freedom, and enjoy the types of professional and personal successes they've always wanted...what I call the Ideal Business – and these lessons can do the same for you too. Dedicated To Your Success,

Pat Rigsby

1

Ideal Business

The 5 Core Components of an Ideal Business

Here is my take on what the characteristics of an 'Ideal Business' are...

Independent - An Ideal Business is controlled by you. That's why you went into business...to be in control of your own destiny. You want the autonomy to build the business that you want.

Distinctive - The Dictionary says Distinctive means *having a special quality, style, attractiveness, etc.; notable.* Do you know any businesses that you'd consider extraordinary that don't fit that description? Your Ideal Business must stand out...it must be *Distinctive.*

Enjoyable - For me this is a huge part of building my Ideal Business. We're all going to spend thousands of hours in our business so being Enjoyable is a must. The business that you construct must be one where you feel like you *get to* go to work most every day...not one where you feel like *you've got to go* to work.

Authentic - Your Ideal Business must be reflective of you, your belief and your values. If you're going to love it, then it can't be cookie cutter and look and feel like every other bland business out there.

Lucrative - Obviously, your Ideal Business needs to be lucrative. You need to be able to enjoy the type of income that provides for both your 'now' and your 'future'.

Your Ideal Business should be all of that and more.

Let's face it, there is no shortage of information on how to build a business available. I'm an Amazon junkie and there are literally thousands of books about 'business', but few are *specifically* written to help a person like me or you. I've read plenty of them and they're written about big corporations and you get to *try* to adapt all that stuff to what you do.

Then there are the solutions that our industry offers...but again, they're more about the person or business creating them and their preferences than they are about you and what you want.

So do yourself (and me) a favor and start thinking about what your **Ideal Business** looks like:

- Who do you want to work with?
- What sort of format will you deliver your training in?
- What type of experience do you want your clients immersed in?
- What type of culture will your facility have? Will it even be a facility or are you going to have an online business?
- How much income will you generate?
- What will your work schedule be?

Start thinking about it...

The Blueprint

If you want to build your Ideal Business you need to:

1. Know who you really want to work with.

2. Get in front of those people...showing them what your business stands for.

3. Get them to know, like and trust you.

4. Ask them to become clients.

5. Over deliver like crazy...giving them what they want and giving them more than they expected.

Below is a simple plan that you can use to dial in your business model...one that will help you simplify things and I've used my business as an example...

1. Decide what you'll be known for.

For me it's building Ideal Businesses and providing World Class Coaching. That's the core of the result I want to deliver (Ideal Business) and the experience (coaching vs simply delivering information) that sets my business apart. What do YOU want to be known for?

2. Decide who you want to know you…your Market.

I want to be known by fitness entrepreneurs.

Who do you want to be known by?

3. Decide at least 3 ways that you'll connect with your Perfect Prospects within that market.

For me it's FB Ads, Speaking and Networking/JV's. It's a combination of meeting fitness entrepreneurs where they are and playing to my strengths.

If I were you I'd choose my three from this list:
- Networking
- FB Ads
- Public Speaking
- Joint Ventures
- Referral/Relationship Marketing
- Direct Mail

4. Decide how you'll deliver the results your Perfect Prospects are looking for.

For me it's Virtual Fitness Mastermind, Courses like the Producer Challenge, my Mastermind & Private Consulting.

So basically it's all coaching driven offerings…usually in a group setting.

If I were you I'd choose my Primary Offering from this list:
- Group Training–8 or more clients.
- Team Training –5-8 clients.
- Semi-Private Training– 2-4 clients.
- One on One Training.

5. Decide how you'll price your services.

For me it's all about providing 10X the value for the investment. So I'm not the highest priced offering…I'm not trying to extract every penny possible from my clients. But I'm not the lowest priced offering either. I'd fall into the 'mid-level priced' offerings – and it's a combination of knowing who I want to work with, what their budget is and my ability to provide 10X value.

So, will you be the:
- Low-Priced Offering
- Mid-Priced Offering
- Premium-Priced Offering

With any of these, the goal is to provide great value for the investment and to do enough volume to meet your financial goals.

So go through these 5 steps to dial things in…

If you do that you'll have a much clearer means of viewing your business and be focused on what really drives your business forward.

So I've spoken a lot about building your Ideal Business over the past several months.

Not someone else's brand or a model you need to squeeze yourself into like a square peg in a round hole.

Well, I spent yesterday with a consulting client who's only 3 months into their business and they just had their first 10K month and think are trending in the right direction in a big way.

So I wanted to make sure some things were addressed so he could have his own Ideal Business. I basically provided a framework and we found his best solutions for each. Here's a general overview of the framework that you can use:

Your Ideal Business Framework...

Your Brand Identity - What will you be known for? Why will people choose you?

Your Client Attraction Plan - Where are those Perfect Prospects and how will you connect with them and draw them to your business?

Your Conversion Plan - How will you convert them into Clients?

Your Service & Experience Plan - How will you get them the results they want and make them feel connected to your business?

Your Business Management & Operations Plan - How will you run your business so that it doesn't run you? How will you make sure that you're profitable? How will you hire and develop staff?

Your Personal Income & Security Plan - How will you reach your income goals? How will you make sure your family has the security you need to provide them (health insurance, life insurance, retirement planning, etc.)?

Your Personal Lifestyle Plan - How will you build and optimize your business so that you are spending the bulk of your time doing the things you are best at, enjoy most and most well suited to do?

How will you create a schedule that gives you freedom but still works to run a successful business?

If you want to create your Ideal Business, you MUST address all of these. Honestly, I don't know of anyone else who talks about them all together but me...but I wanted to share the list so that you can address them all however you choose.

I'll say it again now and I'll say it until you're sick of hearing it:

You can have your **Ideal Business**.

There may be people in your life telling you otherwise...but honestly, it's just because they don't have it and don't have a clue how to get it.

You do.

Don't settle.

The TRUTH about Building an Ideal Business

I often get questions from entrepreneurs about building their Ideal Businesses.

They've usually had someone tell them that it was a fantasy...that they should settle for having what I'd consider a pretty mediocre business.

So I wanted to make sure you knew what I shared with them...

You can build your Ideal Business.

Now, you can't just 'have' your Ideal Business.

It's earned. It's built.

So what's an Ideal Business?

Well, let's start with what it's not…

…It's not a business that's likely going to have you lying on a beach with a laptop and a margarita like you'll see on the cover of some of those books on being a 'lifestyle entrepreneur'.

…It's not exclusive to online or offline businesses.

…It's not a four-hour workweek.

Frankly, I don't know how to build something that doesn't require work. I'm not sure I know anyone that does.

So if that's not an Ideal Business, what is?

First…an Ideal Business is one that allows you to work with the people you want to work with. You should be training the people you want to…the people you are the best at training.

You should be employing the people that you feel are good ambassadors for your business.

And you should be contracting the people that you feel make you better and enjoy working with. From the accountant you hire to the business coach you work with…they should be aligned with your vision.

So that's the 'people piece' of building your Ideal Business.

When it comes to the 'what you do' piece of building your Ideal Business, you decide what you want to be known for.

There's no 'one-size-fits all' path.

If you want to run groups or bootcamps...you decide.

If you want to train in-home or one-on-one, you decide.

Warehouse or retail.

Premium pricing or value pricing.

Fat loss or sports performance.

Who you want to train, how you want to train them...how you're positioned in the market.

You decide.

And when you want to scale your business, you can do it through growing one location, adding other locations, going online and even licensing or franchising.

If you want to grow by having more clients, by having more employees or having more locations...that's up to you.

How you scale the impact you have is up to you.

Now the things that everyone focuses on as soon as I say 'Ideal Business' are Income and Lifestyle...and you decide about those too.

First, they're largely a product of the choices you make with everything else.

And if you want more income...you focus more on being a producer.

If you want Saturdays off, you block them off the schedule and make it work.

You're not a victim.

Your life is not a product of your business...your business is a product of your choices.

So when someone tells you that you can't have your Ideal Business, what they're really telling you is that you're not capable of making good choices and following through to make them a reality.

Screw them.

Your business is a reflection of you. The impact you want to have. The life you want to lead.

Shaping it into your Ideal Business isn't easy...but why would you settle for anything less?

8 Guiding Principles of the Ideal Business

Creating your Ideal Business starts with you.

What you believe. What you want. What you do.

So to help you on the path toward having the business you want, I've provided 8 Guiding Principles.

1. Change Your Focus.

Changing your focus could be your most important challenge.

Most fitness business owners focus on getting by. They think about what tactic will be the Band-Aid they need for today's problem. They think that the magic is in some new training or marketing tactic.

Instead, to create your Ideal Business you must focus on:

- Your VISION.
- Your IMPACT.
- Your PURPOSE.
- Your VALUES.
- The PROBLEMS you'll SOLVE.
- The VALUE you'll ADD in other's lives.
- Your GOALS.
- The ACTION you'll take.

2. Think BIG.

Focus on your VISION. Your Biggest Goals. The Impact you'll have. If you believe you already think BIG... then think even BIGGER!

What would your Ideal Business look like?

The quantity of the effort it takes to just get by is not much different than the quantity of the effort needed to do something extraordinary.

Which will you choose to think about?

3. Operate Differently.

Your business is perfectly designed to get the results you're getting today. If you want a different outcome…you must do things differently.

Abandon the mediocre and be better.

If you want to be known as #1 in your market…then you better operate the way a #1 should.

4. Take Massive Action.

To make more progress in the next 6 months than you've made in the last 6 years…you must take massive action.

No little tweaks.

Don't talk about what you'll do or just 'dip your toe in the water'…dive in headfirst. Action creates momentum.

Decide what 3 massive actions you could take right now that would create a quantum leap in your business.

Then act!

5. Success is a Team Sport.

Find people that connect with your vision. Clients. Team Members. Friends.

Focus on attitude. Attract energy givers…not energy takers. Coach them up. Lead and bring out the best in others.

No one builds their Ideal Business alone.

6. Simple = Successful.

Simple executed well ALWAYS beats complex executed in a mediocre way.

Be the best at a few things. Leave the rest to others to be the best at. Be the best for a few people. Leave the rest for others to help.

Stay in your lane and play to your strengths.

7. Focus on Relationships.

Maximize the relationships in your life. Connect deeply and often. Care about people when others see them as nothing more than a means to an end.

Help enough people reach their goals and you'll reach yours.

8. Be a Producer.

Everything in your business…in your life…take responsibility for Producing.

- Results and experiences for clients.
- Culture and fulfillment for your team.
- Revenue and profit for your business.
- Income, impact and freedom for you.

If you want to build your Ideal Business…you must Produce.

"The mind, once expanded to dimensions of larger ideas, never returns to its original size."

—Oliver Wendell Holmes

Be ruthless about being different and being better. Ordinary businesses exist because we settle for ordinary thoughts and actions.

3 Things You Can Do

As you may know by now, I was a college baseball coach, and you may have heard me mention a number of times before – coaching taught me a lot.

Because we were a program with pretty limited resources I had to learn how to achieve success by doing some things differently than the competition since we weren't going to compete by having more scholarships (we had about 1/10 the number our best competitors had) or a nicer facility (we used a city owned park).

So I read books on business and marketing as well as the typical coaching fare – looking for an advantage.

Here are three strategies which allowed us to become a nationally competitive program in spite of resources that were better suited for a high school team and that I have used to help us achieve similar success in business:

Find Opportunity Where Others Don't – In baseball, coaches typically allocate a lot of their scholarship money for pitchers and shortstops. They invest a lot of practice time on things like pickoff plays and obscure bunt defenses. In truth - except for a select few they all do the same stuff.

Not me.

We weren't going to outspend our competition for the pitchers they wanted – so I focused my energies on aggressively going after players with great offensive potential that were undervalued by the competition and just tried to find diamonds in the rough when it came to pitchers or shortstops. When it came to practice time – instead of spending much time on things that happen 5% of the time in the game I dedicated our practices to 3 things:

1. The things that happen most of the time in games. The basics.

2. Making our players better athletes. We took an approach to strength & conditioning that was as aggressive as most football programs while most other teams were still using Nautilus machines.

3. We approached our skill development strategy in a way that really deviated from the norm.

Sounds kind of obvious, but it's certainly an outlier in baseball.

Transitioning to my first training business – this approach led me to gravitate toward 30 minute 1 on 1 sessions, group based training and EFT billing all the way back in 2004.

Now it's teaching fitness entrepreneurs to build their Ideal Business while everyone else either just teaches marketing tactics or asks you to fit into their model of what your business should be.

To apply this in your own business – look at what others don't do or don't do well. Be a specialist. Target a gap in the market or approach how you impact your area in a different way. Create a unique experience. Avoid average.

There are undervalued opportunities in EVERY business and EVERY market – it's your job to find them.

Play To Your Strengths – Once I identified a formula that worked for building our team – I just expanded on it. I worked on recruiting an even better caliber of player that fit the same mold. I kept refining the system.

I didn't try to also do all the things the competitors were doing. I simply wanted to create the best possible version of our organization.

In the business world, this means, don't try to be all things to all people. Pick a couple of things and be extraordinary at them. When it comes to marketing – hone in on 2-3 core systems and work them aggressively every day until your business is where you want.

Again - be a specialist. Choose an approach to marketing that fits your strengths. Build a culture that matches your personality. If your business is built around your strengths it will be far, far easier to stand out from the crowd.

Get Personal – My biggest strength as a coach was as a recruiter. And my recruiting was simple:

1. Create a 'product' (our program) players would want to be a part of.

2. Build and cultivate relationships with the players that would be a good fit for what we were trying to do.

So I made a LOT of personal calls. A lot of visits to get to know people. I went to tons of coaching clinics to build relationships with the high school coaches. I took the prospects and their families on tours when they came to campus instead of delegating it. If getting the right players was the most important factor in being successful – then getting personal was my way of doing it.

Business is the same. I asked attendees at a recent workshop how many of them had my personal phone number…most all did. I asked the same thing about a few of my competitors...zero hands.

Private consulting takes place at my home office. I try like crazy to personally connect with people as much as I can.

If you want to see an immediate uptick in your business – take every interaction you make up one level:
- If you normally send a mass email – send a personal one.
- If you normally send a personal email – make a call.
- If you normally make a call – visit in person.

I guarantee you'll love the results.

OK – 3 lessons learned from coaching college baseball that have continued to help me time and time again in business. They've all worked well for me – now let them work for you.

3 Rules for Building the Business YOU Want

A while back, Holly and I spoke at the Nor-Cal Fitness Summit and that speaking engagement was a great example of three rules or guardrails that are critical if you want to build your Ideal Business.

I thought this trip would be a great opportunity to share 3 rules that I follow to build my Ideal Business that you should be following too.

Rule #1 - You Decide What You'll Do And What You Won't.

It's your business so you should decide which clients you'll take, what hours you'll train, how you'll market, how you should price your services and everything in between.

For me, speaking at the Nor-Cal Fitness Summit was a cool opportunity that the hosts and I have been trying to make happen for a while but my schedule never fit.

Well this time it was only going to fit if Holly could come, as her birthday fell on the weekend of the event.

So Holly came along and presented too.

If she couldn't have made the trip, I'd have passed. Family first is a 'rule' for me.

Now I get that if your business is just getting started you might take on a few clients to pay the bills or make some sacrifices that you don't really want to make forever…I know I did.

But you need to map out your Rules and work toward sticking to them or you'll be running a start-up business forever.

Rule #2 - Market Smart.

I'll admit it, I really enjoy marketing and selling. I think of it like a game that I'm always trying to improve at playing.

But part of the reason I enjoy marketing is that I know how to market smart.

See, marketing smart really centers around 2 things…

- Fishing where the fish are.
- Making sure your message will speak to the prospects you want to attract.

The Nor-Cal Fitness Summit was a perfect example.

Motivated fitness professionals who are excited about getting better at what they do…that's pretty much my target market.

To make it even better…of the speakers, the following have worked for me, been coaching clients or worked with me:

- Luka Hocevar
- AJ Roberts
- Corey Taylor
- Seth Munsey
- Holly Rigsby
- Brian Grasso

That's half the lineup.

So attendees who were excited about hearing them are more likely to be interested in what I'd have to offer.

And my message will be about building your Ideal Business. So getting in front of the right people and talking about what I do that is different…that's smart marketing.

How can you do that?

Referrals are the right people.

You can target on Facebook.

You can show how you are different time and time again through web copy, the social proof you use, talks you give, how you educate clients and staff to talk about you and so on.

Rule #3 - Play To Your Strengths.

I know my strengths…and there aren't too many.

Networking/Relationship Marketing
Coaching
Marketing/Selling/Producing
Writing
Business Development/Business Optimization

So an opportunity like the Nor-Cal Summit plays to most of these.

I'll be able to network and its presenting format that will allow me to coach and be more informal. As a speaker, I'm fine there…I'm not as good in a really polished setting.

I'll be talking about the things I enjoy and am good at.

I'll try to move attendees to my newsletter so I can play to my writing strength.

I try to build my business so that most of my time is spent on this stuff. Probably 90%.

You should do the same…figure out what you do well or want to learn to do well…then build around it. Systematize, minimize, delegate or eliminate the rest.

Those are 3 rules I live by when it comes to business. I know how important they are to me…I suspect they'll be just as valuable to you too.

Is Your Business Making You Happy?

One year after selling my stake in my previous companies and starting anew, Holly and I attended an event in San Diego that allowed me to have some time to reflect on year one and how happy that shift allowed me to be with my business.

I think we're all striving for that - right?

We all want to feel like we GET to go to work rather than that we've GOT to go to work.

And while I won't try to tell you that every minute of my new business venture has been a blast (a lot of the transition stuff in the first couple of months was just really, really tedious) I want to share the things that I've focused on that have helped me really have as much fun professionally as I've ever had so you can employ them too:

1. Work with the clients you enjoy.

There is a direct correlation between the people you accept as clients or the people you work closely with and your day to day happiness.

For me - I'd rather part ways with a client...be it a private client or a member of Virtual Fitness Mastermind...than keep them around if I don't enjoy them.

In fact, if someone asks to cancel VFM I've grown to actually be pleased with it because if they don't want to build their Ideal Business and don't feel connected to our community - I really don't want folks like that around.

They may be great people...but they're not the right people.

2. Play to your strengths.

I don't want you to think that you don't ever have to do things that you don't like...frankly I don't enjoy the time away from my family when I travel (so it's great that Holly came on that trip with me) or some of the details of project management...but I've built my business and 90% of how I spend my time around the things I do enjoy...coaching, creation, business strategy, marketing, sales, writing, networking and business development.

I do other things...but a very high percentage of my time is on these things...and even when I'm doing the stuff I don't enjoy (being away from my family) it's because I'm doing things or improving at things just listed.

3. Actively work to avoid and eliminate the things you don't like.

This may be the most important of all. We all (hopefully) are trying to attract the right clients, do the things we like, etc... But are we really pruning away the stuff we don't want in our business?

If there are clients we don't want...are we severing ties?

Are we crafting our marketing to avoid attracting more of them?

Are we making our programs really reflective of what we want to be known for or are we tolerating just selling 'stuff"?

Are we collaborating with people we don't enjoy?

Doing a lot of tasks that stress us out?

I think that purging as much of the things you don't like from your business is an act that can probably bring you as much professional happiness as anything you can do.

While there are plenty of other things that I think make you or I happy in business...we should both start with those 3.

And I don't want you to think for a minute that I've got the market cornered on this 'Ideal Business' or business that makes me happy thing.

I've seen a lot of my friends and clients do the same.

And you can too.

But it won't happen by accident.

Like anything worth having, you must pursue it aggressively.

But it's worth it...that I can promise you.

What Do You Love?

What do you like about your business?

For me it's a few things…

- I love coaching.

- I love connecting.

- I love writing.

- I love problem solving.

- I love creating.

What about you?

What do you love about your business?

Not what you kind of enjoy…like or tolerate.

Love.

Now there are some things in my business that I'm just 'ok' with…

- Operations

 - Administrative Work

 - Financial / Accounting Work

 And stuff that I just plain dislike…

 - Travel without my family.

 That's it.

I've systematically moved most of my business into that 'love' category, gotten comfortable with the 'ok' category by focusing on the key parts as it relates to what I do and finding great help for the rest…

…and the last category, I just try to minimize.

I travel several times a year to present, where I often get to see friends, connect with some new people and share my message…but, at this point in my life, I head home as soon as I can.

No extra days to sightsee, even when it's somewhere new. I only want to experience those new sights with my family.

I share this with you because I want you to recognize that how we operate our business is a series of choices…choices that we each make.

I've made a bunch to try to do more of what I love and less of stuff I don't.

Some things I won't stop or let go of completely because the benefit is big or I think my business as a whole operates better and as a whole makes me happier with me handling certain things…but again, those are choices.

Very few of the choices to focus on doing my top 5-10% of activities and making my business more family and personal life friendly were giant, sweeping ones…mostly just a bunch of smaller ones, day after day.

And the way you run your business is based on your choices too.

If you work on Saturday, it's a choice.

If you don't hire and empower good people…it's a choice.

To sell or not to sell.

To market or not to market.

It's all a choice.

You started your business and you're not a victim of it.

You just have to make the choices that will lead where you want to go…one by one.

So what choice are you going to make to improve your business today?

The Grass is Greener Where You Water It...

One of my favorite consulting trips in recent memory was a little different. It was with a college baseball program. One of the top programs in the country...and it was easy to see why.

The Head Coach and his staff have approached running their program differently than every other program I've been around or seen.

I won't get into details as they have developed some distinct competitive advantages and I'll leave the decision to them as to how much they want to share.

But I will tell you this...it was impressive.

They saw what everyone else was doing and didn't just blindly follow the leader.

They constantly are looking for different, better ways to build their program.

And this approach has helped them ascend to arguably being one of the top 10 programs in the country at a (really great) University that you've likely never heard of.

But while other coaches who have some success are always looking for the next, higher profile job...the proverbial 'grass is always greener on the other side' mentality...this coach and his staff have simply focused on making their own grass green to the point that their current program is no longer a stepping stone - rather it's a destination location.

There are so many lessons from how they've built this program that I could share that would be very applicable to what you do...but I'll focus on a select few:

1. Quit chasing the next shiny object and focus on just getting better at what you do...every day.

2. Focus on improving from the inside - out. They're great at developing the players they have and helping them maximize their potential. Most competitors aren't.

3. Attract people who are a great fit. Build a culture that appeals to your ideal prospect and really focus on attracting them rather than just chasing everyone.

4. Beat the competition by being different and being better. Don't be a 'me too' business...but don't just settle for being different...still strive to be great at what you do.

Again, I could go on and on...but this consulting session just really reinforced to me that all the things I talk about regarding building your Ideal Business are the real path to follow...all the way down to making sure your job really allows you to have the lifestyle you want.

The Head Coach, Dan, is a father of five and really has built things so that his family can be involved and it seems like the entire situation he's created is the college baseball version of his Ideal Business.

Really awesome to see and exciting to once again be reminded that if you're willing to do the work you can construct a tremendously successful career that helps you achieve all your goals.

If you're not already on the path to having this type of career or business...do yourself a favor and do what it takes to start moving toward having your Ideal Business (or your professional equivalent of that) today. There is nothing you can do professionally that will provide you any greater satisfaction.

What Everyone Else Seems to Miss…

When I started my new business, I began talking about building your Ideal Business.

Sure, I'd mentioned it prior to that - but I'd never really made it my primary focus.

But, ultimately, I wanted to really spend my time working on what I'm most passionate about…and that's it.

See, I think your Ideal Business is simply the business YOU want.

The one that allows you to help the clients you want to help in the way you want to help them…

…but also the business that allows you to live the life YOU want to live.

And that's the part I felt that everyone else was missing.

As a business owner, the line that divides your business life and your personal life gets blurry.

And everything that I've come across both in our industry and outside of it focuses on how to map out strategies and systems for your business…but they ignore YOU.

Why are you helping everyone else reach their goals while you ignore yours?

When I ask people what their goals are I usually get answers like:

I want 200% more clients.

I want to increase my monthly revenue by $10,000 per month.

I want a bigger facility.

But that is only part of the equation.

I want to know things like:

What you want your personal income to be.

I want to be at home 10 more hours per week.

How much you want to save for retirement this year.

Where and how long you want to vacation.

The house you want to buy and how much you need to save for a down payment.

As a fitness entrepreneur you deserve all of it.

But you have to go get it. You have to produce it.

But before that you need to decide.

Decide what you want for your business and for YOU.

Be specific.

What do you want YOUR business to be known for?

Who are YOUR perfect clients?

How many clients, how much revenue do YOU want?

How do YOU want to train?

How much do YOU want to make (present income and money you save)?

How do you want YOUR schedule to look (your weekly schedule, your vacations)?

DECIDE.

Then the job is to PRODUCE it.

In truth…it's that simple.

And those are the areas I wanted to focus my business on…to help YOU get clear on your Ideal Business and to help you PRODUCE it.

In my opinion, that's what you should be spending all of your work time on…yet I feel like most everyone else misses this. They get caught up in tactics or systems…but they forget:

The destination (your Ideal Business).

The engine to get you there (your Production).

Your job is to be one of the select few that do understand, embrace and live these simple but powerful ideas.

So I'll end by asking you to start your week to consider these 2 questions:

Are you clear on what YOUR Ideal Business is?

Are you actively PRODUCING that business and everything which goes into it now?

If you are…wonderful.

If you aren't…well you can lean on me to coach you through both of those. That's my Ideal Business.

Do You "Have To"?

So I was having a conversation with my best friend a few days ago and we were talking about our careers.

Well, he not only has a career that he's incredibly good at, but he also really enjoys it.

But he did share the one drawback.

He said…

"I spend about 80% of my time doing things I *have to* do and 20% of my time doing what I *want to* do. My goal is to spend the 80% doing what I want to do and the 20% doing what I *have to* do."

Sound familiar?

I know it does for me.

With my last business that enjoyed quite a lot of success, I eventually was spending most of my time doing the things I had to do and not nearly enough time doing what I enjoyed doing.

I hear it from fitness entrepreneurs each and every day too.

It's not that they don't want to still train any clients in most cases.

They want to be able to choose.

They don't want to be handcuffed to doing things, training all hours of the day and being saddled with everything from being the bookkeeper, office manager and salesperson to training clients, program design and being the janitor.

They want to do what they're best at and what has the most impact…and find ways to minimize, outsource or systemize the rest.

I've been engineering my business to address this. Working to create my Ideal Business.

At this point I'd say I'm right around that 80/20 ratio.

80% of my time is doing what I *want to* do and 20% doing what I*have to* do.

I've spent more *want to* time in the first 6 months of my current business than in the final 3 years of my previous business…but that really is about a decision not to settle.

A decision that each of us can make…each and every day.

So ask yourself…what percentage of your time is spent on *want to* activities?

And if the number isn't as high as you'd like…ask yourself just one more question:

What are you going to do about it?

3 Easy Questions to Grow Your Ideal Business

If you want to grow your business you need to be able to successfully answer these 3 questions:

Who do you want to work with?

Where can you find them?

How will you serve them?

Let's break it down…

Who do you want to work with?

Do you want to work with busy moms?

Baby boomers?

Baseball players?

Clients of a certain income?

Age range?

Gender?

Experienced exercisers or novices?

You pick. If you're going to be spending 20-40 hours per week training those clients then you need to work to build your business around who you want rather than just taking anyone with a pulse and a credit card.

For Holly, it's busy moms who want to workout at home.

For me it's fitness entrepreneurs.

Who is it for you?

Where can you find them?

Where can you find the people you want to work with? It's simpler than it may seem at first thought. You likely have some of these clients in your business already…so figure out where they are when they're not with you.

What neighborhood do they live in?

What are their interests?

Where do they work?

What other businesses do they frequent?

Can you find them online (yes)? Where?

For me…it starts online since most of the points of entry to my business are online. Facebook, LinkedIn, other sites and people who have fitness entrepreneurs in their audience. After that it's usually live industry events where I can meet people in person and connect with them.

For Holly it's largely places like Facebook, Pinterest and YouTube since her business is entirely online.

And then once you know who they are and where to find them…

How will you serve them?

Is in through groups?

Team training?

Semi-private?

One-on-one?

Online training?

With a product or a membership site?

You decide. How do you want to help them reach their goals?

For Holly – serving them starts with a product that teaches them her approach to looking and feeling the way they want in the time they have and then for the people who are the right fit…it's a membership community where she provides online coaching.

For me, it starts with Virtual Fitness Mastermind to provide the tools, strategies and tactics in conjunction with a private community…then a couple of intensive courses to be more focused and interactive…and finally private consulting and masterminds so I can spend more time in person with those perfect clients.

That's exactly how I want to work with my clients…how do you want to work with yours?

You have to answer these questions if you're going to build your Ideal Business. It's a must.

Sure – once you do, you'll have to make sure you craft a message that reflects you well and attracts them…and you will want to make sure that you're delivering the results and experience they want…but start with these.

Get clear on them.

Decide what you want…then produce that outcome.

Experts vs. Opportunists

One of the biggest problems I see today is people trying to be opportunists.

It first became noticeable to me when I started getting involved in the online business side of things and saw countless people pretending to be experts in things they had little if any true experience in.

They saw an opportunity to make some quick money and went after it.

I see it with fitness pros all the time too.

They read about someone doing well with youth fitness or corporate fitness and the next thing you know that person is a youth fitness or corporate fitness expert. (Apparently – if you call yourself an expert it must be true…ugh.)

Find out what you're good at and what you've proven to do well…and build a brand around it.

I bought Dan John's new book, *Can You Go* and read it beginning to end…he's a very, very good writer.

In the book, he talks about never teaching something he's not done. He talked about a 10,000 swing challenge he did and then wrote an article about…within minutes there were dozens of people telling him how to do it better.

But they were talking theory…they hadn't done it.

Then yesterday, I also saw something about a product someone created that they basically admitted that they'd just read a bunch of stuff and recycled it…and then are going to try to sell it. Geez.

I'm guessing that the businesses that you admire are built off of someone or some group of people being great at what they do…not just seeing an opportunity in the market to make a quick buck.

I know that I do.

There is something to be learned from that…

If you become great at what you do and get at least moderately proficient at letting the world know who you're for, what problems you solve better than other people and the results you get…people will actually seek you out.

But if you simply jump from thing to thing trying to be an instant expert instead of building a deserved identity for being really good at something…you'll never be a trusted authority.

So how can you use this to be better?

Two ways really…

1. When you're learning from someone…make sure they've enjoyed proven success doing what they teach. They're not just recycling something someone else said or what they think is 'hot.'

Studying proven success will not only be more likely to work for you – but we're all a product of what we surround ourselves with, so if you want to build a business brand that stands out by being the best…then you need to surround yourself with others who do the same.

2. Spend more time trying to be great at and be known for one thing instead of chasing every shiny object. You can't be legitimate and be an expert in one thing this week, another thing next week and another thing the week after that.

Own a segment of your market instead of trying to 'chase a quick buck.'

I understand the lure of being an Opportunist…but opportunists are often figured out by the market as being all sizzle and no steak.

That's why they're off to the next opportunity…because the last one didn't work or they got 'found out' as being what they really are.

Don't be that. It's easy…but if something is easy – it's probably not great.

Instead, strive to become an expert. (It's not easy...but it's worth it.)

Do what it takes to become one and get good at letting the market know what you do and who it's for.

That's the core of building your Ideal Business.

Playing to Your Strengths

Not too long ago, I was asked to speak at an event where I was given 18 minutes to present.

Most of the talks I do are 45-60 minutes, so when I was told this was more like a TED talk, I thought for a while about what one big idea I wanted to share.

I thought about what has helped me the most...and what I've witnessed being the most critical factor for so many others successes.

Once I used that as my filter it became clear...

Play to Your Strengths.

Every time I've struggled with something it's been a direct result of trying to be someone I'm not...either I was trying to emulate someone else or I let myself be pushed to do things that were not in my areas of strength.

But at the same time...*every,* without exception, *every* great success I've had has hinged on me doing one or more of the small number of things I do well.

But it's not just me.

Look at anyone you admire...anyone who has enjoyed some success.

They're not just a clone of someone else. They aren't just doing what everyone else does.

They aren't a follower.

They lead.

They're authentic.

They're playing to their strengths.

So my suggestion to you is to:

First...figure out what you do well or are willing to commit to becoming great at.

Focus most of your efforts on those things...build your business with those strengths at the centerpiece.

Then - for the things that your business requires that fall outside those strengths...do one of 3 things...eliminate it, minimize it or empower someone else to do it.

If all you do is settle for trying to emulate someone else...you'll always be mediocre.

But if you go all in to building around the gifts, talents, experiences and strengths you have...you'll be laying the foundation for greatness.

The choice is yours. What will you do?

Do You Have These?

If you want to enjoy the type of business success that I suspect you do...then you're going to need to create your own rules.

See, most of us get into business because we don't want to follow someone else's rules. We either aren't happy or feel like the ceiling is just too low.

Then, most of the time what happens is one of these two scenarios...

1. You simply adopt someone else's rules as your own by choice.
2. You fail to ever create your own rules so you're inadvertently controlled by other's rules.

In the first case, you may just follow someone else's franchise or license...or you just piece together rules from a variety of sources.

In the second case you're so hell-bent on being your own individual you don't even bother to set your own rules...so then you're stuck being controlled by everyone else's set of rules whether you realize it or not.

So what I propose to you is this:

Create your own rules.

That's pretty much why I created PatRigsby.com and the concept of your Ideal Business.

Because you need to have rules that you run your business by...

...but they should be your *own*.

To be successful in life, you have to follow some rules.

You need rules point out the most direct route to where you want to go.

"Do this."

"Don't do that."

Make enough right choices and you'll have the business that you want.

Back in my coaching career I followed the typical rules and we were average...but when I created my own we became a championship caliber program.

As a business owner - when I've been able to craft my own rules I've enjoyed success and been happy...and when I've tried to simply fit into someone else's...well, not so good.

So now, I know.

I have rules that I use to guide my direction and to make my decisions.

If I veer from them much at all, I'm essentially saying that my Ideal Business isn't important to me.

Doesn't matter if it's more money, bigger opportunities or anything else.

I'm either playing by my rules or someone else's.

In fact, I've recognized that I'm playing by someone's rules 100% of the time...and my goal is to progressively move toward that being 100% mine and 0% someone else's.

This doesn't mean I can't work with others or even have business partners.

It means that I need to be doing my stuff by my rules if they're going to get the best version of me and if I'm going to be happy.

So here's what I want to leave you with:

You can have the business that you want...but only if you create your own rules and play by them.

P.S. - Here are a couple of my rules if this helps get you started:

1. Family first. This starts with time and how I spend it...but it really permeates everything I do.

2. Do what I'm good at and what I enjoy. Other stuff has to get done...but I systematically work to minimize it or outsource it if it doesn't fit that criteria.

3. Work only with people who make me happy...and the closer I work with someone the more this is a focus. So if you're a MM member or private client you can trust that I really like you.

The further I get into my business and the more financial autonomy I have...the more rigid these become. I assure you that especially with #2 & #3...these were not always in place. It's a process.

Think Big

Over time I've come across so many people who had more talent than I can imagine having.

People who picked up things easily, were great communicators and just seemed to be good at everything they've tried.

But so many of them settle for average results...average businesses...even average lives because they never get clear about what they want.

With a vision for what success looks like to you...what I call your Ideal Business...that success comes much more easily.

Focus on your Ideal Business...that vision that excites you. Focus on it exclusively. Hang onto it regardless of the people who try to tear it down.

Please know this:

If you don't have a dream of your own, you'll work all your life to fulfill someone else's dream.

Also know that thinking big about what your Ideal Business is costs you nothing, while not doing it will cost you virtually everything professionally.

Without this vision you cannot have a meaningful goal.

Without a goal you'll never take any positive action.

Without any positive action, nothing will happen to bring you any closer to your Ideal Business.

And if you're going to aim, you may as well aim high.

The bigger your vision for your Ideal Business is, the more excited and motivated you will be to actually begin on the road to reaching it.

A clear vision for what we want motivates us and keeps us going when things get difficult.

If you always have that vision of your Ideal Business in mind, you'll make the right decisions that will take you closer to your goal.

James Collins and Jerry Pores, in their book *Built To Last*, describe corporate success as stemming from "Big Hairy Audacious Goals."

It's the same for us small business owners - if you think big, you win big.

Beware of the Dream Killers.

As kids we naturally have wild and wonderful imaginations and can easily picture how our lives could be.

We all have the capacity to "make believe" and build a dream world for ourselves.

But as we grow older, we unfortunately and inevitably run into some very dangerous people.

The Dream Killers.

Dream Killers are everywhere.

They are the people who constantly tell us we cannot do things, that we should be careful "not to fail."

These people may be our friends, relatives, parents, or coaches.

They may be total strangers.

We have to be vigilant and ensure they don't influence our thinking in any way.

Instead - try to find dream builders – positive, successful people – to be with.

And where you can't avoid Dream Killers, build barriers to keep your vision safe.

So Decide Where You Want To Go...

Direction is central to creating your Ideal Business.

When you have your vision, you can then decide in what direction you're headed.

Translate your Ideal Business into some easily definable short-term goals in a series of easy-to-accomplish steps that you can grasp and complete.

Refer to your vision and the steps you need to accomplish every day.

Do not be afraid to share these with people you trust to be supportive, to help guide you.

Start talking to people about how to reach your goals.

All these things make your goals more real.

They make your commitment real, rather than just being something buried in your head that you can easily forget.

This is where more people we know go wrong.

They don't get clear about what they want.

Without making that choice, people end up with whatever life gives them.

And that is rarely if ever what anyone would consider Ideal.

Set clear, realistic goals.

Goals provide focus and directions, and with them many things that seem difficult become simple.

With clear goals, the steps to your success often seem to just fall into place.

Without your target...that Ideal Business, it can be impossible to decide what you need to do.

Are You Willing to Pay the Price?

When you have your vision for what your Ideal Business looks like, figure out what price you'll have to pay to achieve it.

Everything worthwhile has some sort of price you must invest.

Time, effort, commitment.

Decide now what you are willing to give up to achieve your goal, then pay that price and pay it without hesitation or regret.

Because if you think big enough and decide what your Ideal Business really looks like - the investment you make will give you a better return than you ever could have imagined.

The 80/20 Life

By now you understand the 80/20 principle…that 20 percent of your effort will yield 80 of your results.

Personally, when I developed the concept of creating the Ideal Business it really centered around that principle.

Focusing on the 20% of things in your business or life that are most important to you…the ones that bring success and happiness into your life.

Instead of trying to be good at everything, focusing on your areas of strength and greatest impact.

Instead of letting your time be controlled by people that just don't matter that much to you, taking control of your time to invest it with the people you enjoy most…your family, your friends and those clients you want to serve.

Choosing how you spend your day…treating it just like money, so yes,'spend or invest' instead of just managing your day and reacting.

Understanding that not everything is of equal importance.

Just because someone has your phone number doesn't mean they get your time.

Just because someone has your email address doesn't mean you have to read what they send.

Just because someone wants something or a task may need to be done doesn't mean that you have to do it.

You don't need to be good or even average at everything.

Why not be great at the 20% that allows you to build the business and the life that you want?

Trying to be all things to all people, whether it's in your business or your personal life…is a recipe for mediocrity at best and disaster at worst.

So focus on doing what you do best, has the greatest impact and moves you toward the life and the business you want.

That's the 80/20 life.

Building My Business: Lessons You Can Apply

Building PatrickRigsby.com, I've followed the same principles or concepts that I teach the people I work with. Because of that I thought I'd give you some examples of what I've done with my own business and how you can apply those concepts in your business.

Decide Who You Are For…And Who You're Not – I built PatRigsby.com specifically for high quality fitness and performance entrepreneurs who want to build their Ideal Businesses.

Virtually all the other industry coaching / licensing / franchising solutions that are out there are aiming at a much broader audience. They are not only trying to work with the people I am, but with non-business owners, people outside the fitness industry - the business opportunity crowd, the same people that might buy a Subway, and fitness business owners who just want to make more money or are okay with fitting into someone else's system.

I was very clear from day one with whom I was trying to serve. I don't want business opportunity seekers. I don't want people just trying to make a quick buck. I only want trainers and coaches who are 100% committed to delivering a great service and want the strategy, knowledge, systems and coaching that I can provide to build the Ideal Business that they want.

This means that I have to sometimes turn away business. Fine by me. If someone isn't the right fit, I must turn them away or I eventually lose my ability to attract those who are the right fit.

How You Can Apply This: Determine who your ideal client is and be the best in your market at serving them. Take a look at the people who you currently work with. Who do you love training? Who are your best clients? Start working to attract more of them and (politely) make it clear that those who aren't this type of client aren't really a good fit for your brand.

Choose A Niche And Be The Leader In It– This may seem like it's the same thing as the previous concept, but it's not really. For PatRigsby.com, I wanted to build a business to serve those who seek to build their Ideal Business. I don't really have any interest in being part of the shiny object, marketing hacks crowd or trying to ask you to just fit yourself into my one-size-fits-all approach like a square peg in a round hole.

And, in truth…I only want to be known for these things that fit under that Ideal Business umbrella…so much so that when someone in our industry says them, they think of me:

- Ideal Business
- Production
- Brand Building

- Business Coaching

That's about it.

I feel very strongly that the future of the fitness industry is in alignment with this and the type of people I want to work with fit with this, so I'm committed to building my business centered on those things.

Not to toot my own horn too much, but I immediately jumped to the front of the pack as the market leader for my niche – in part because no one else really focuses on those things I mentioned. There are no solutions focusing on creating an Ideal Business other than me…and really no others that focus on the components I listed either.

How You Can Apply This: So who do you want to serve and how can you be different than everyone else? That's really what it boils down to. Go to any big box gym and you'll find trainers that claim to be experts in fat loss, corrective exercise, post-natal, wedding weight loss, sports performance training and anything else they can tell you to separate you from your money.

Who can you be the specialist for and deliver a service that clearly stands above the competition? What do you love to do? What do you want to be known for?

Figure out what you can be the best at and who you can be the best for and go all in on it.

Provide Solutions To Your Market's Biggest Problems – When I was building my new business I basically wanted to solve the problems the good trainers and coaches in the industry were facing that was preventing them from building the business that they wanted…their Ideal Business.

Some of the common problems were:

- Not knowing where they wanted to go…not getting clear about what their Ideal Business looked like.
- Not having a brand reflective of what they wanted to be known for…one that would attract who they wanted to work with.
- Not being Producers.
- Not having a plan that attracts and converts the **right** clients.
- Not being happy…working hard and not feeling like they're getting what they want in return.
- Not having a coach to bring out the best in them.

There are other problems that fitness entrepreneurs face when building a business but these are what I want to focus on…what comprise my Ideal Business.

How You Can Apply This: So what prevents your clients from reaching their goals?

- A lack of time?
- A lack of knowledge?
- A lack of motivation?
- Simplified solutions to make attaining progress easier?
- Accountability?

Once you get clear on what's holding your Ideal Clients back then your job is simply to give them the solutions they need to get where they want to go.

Not Being 'One Size Fits All' – This is probably where I differ most from other fitness business solutions. When you think of franchising, you think of McDonalds or Subway, right? Everything looks exactly the same. In our world there are plenty of franchises, licenses and programs that take that approach.

I didn't want to be that at all.

I wanted to provide strategies, systems, tools and coaching that allowed my Ideal Clients to build their Ideal Business...with zero regard to my preferences.

I wanted to let them play to their strengths, build on their passions and do the things they could be best at rather than just creating another 'me too' business.

How You Can Apply This: Are you assessing? Are you truly listening to your clients' goals? Are you building their programming around what you discover or are you just trying to fit them into what you do?

Individual needs call for individual solutions.

Even if you run a group program...you don't actually have a group of 20 in a session...you have 1 person who wants to be great 20 times over.

People are important...treat them accordingly.

Connecting – One of the first things I did was invest a lot of time connecting with friends in the industry. Not really asking them for anything…just connecting. Learning how I could help. Asking for their advice and feedback.

This was one of the most rewarding parts of my new venture. In the past I'd been so caught up in what we were doing I wasn't focused enough on what my friends were doing unless it related to the events or projects my company was involved in.

That had never been my approach in the past…but I'd drifted into that approach and I knew that I wanted to change it.

So not only did the connecting rekindle and enhance relationships…it opened doors, created opportunities, allowed me to help friends…and, in truth, was just really fun.

How You Can Apply This: Do the things I've consistently told you to do when it comes to connecting. Reach out to your connections…and not just the people you see in the gym every day or two. Ask how you can help. Ask for advice. Tell them what you're doing. Communicate regularly.

Your business will grow because of it…but you'll have more fun in the process.

Know What You Want – I'll close with this…know what you want. Know what success looks like to you. To me success looked like:

- Putting my family first. Spending time with them on my terms…being able to coach their sports teams, take vacations, share experiences.
- Spending 90% of my time doing the stuff I'm best at and

enjoy most.

- Helping people build their vision instead of just cloning mine.
- Working only with people who make me happy.
- Enjoying income that allowed me to reach my 'today' goals and my 'long term' goals.

How You Can Apply This: This one is pretty straightforward…create a list of what success looks like to you and then start incrementally working toward it. It's not an overnight thing…I was back to building some web pages and doing some tech oriented customer services when I launched – I felt like I needed to do it to get a handle on who I should be hiring. But I've systematically moved toward the things I listed above…step by step. And you can too. Just set a target and go after it…daily.

Hopefully you got some takeaways from this. It's truly an overview of how I started building my Ideal Business and the concepts I've used are the same ones we teach to you.

Key Takeaways

Every year, my family takes a trip or two to Disney World. So, I wanted to share a collection of takeaways that would be actionable in your business…so here goes.

It's All About Experience – Disney World isn't known for the tallest or fastest roller coasters, but the theme and the experience they wrap around the coasters they have are what separates them from the rest. It's really that way with everything they do, from having popular characters in many of the restaurants for visits and pictures to offering 'Fast Passes' so you can circumvent long lines to enjoy your favorite rides.

Disney works tirelessly to maximize the guest's experience – and it's easily their bestselling tool. Over 80% of guests return – and that's at a pretty steep price tag. Outside of return visitors, their best source of traffic is referrals – again, based on the experience they provide.

Your Ideal Business Takeaway: Focus on making the experience your clients have with your business stand above the rest. Remember, they probably aren't experts in your craft so differentiating you solely by your skill as a professional isn't enough. You need to find ways to make certain that they have a more enjoyable time with you than they could with any other fitness solution. Your rewards will be better retention and many more referrals.

Make It Easy – One of my favorite things about trips to Disney World is how easy they make it. From bundling in all the meals into the package and providing transportation to the parks from our resort, to picking up our bags from the airline and letting you check in and check bags at our resort for our trip home.

I travel more than most and by eliminating many of the hassles that go along with travel, Disney has really made it seem like a longer vacation for me rather than me having to deal with a bunch of hassles to eventually get to the resort or get home. To me, this is a huge added value because we want to go to the resort and enjoy the parks. We tolerate the travel – and they make it much, much easier to tolerate.

***Your Ideal Business Takeaway:** What are the hassles your clients have to deal with to do business with you? They have to make that first visit where they feel overwhelmed and a little intimidated. Can you make it more comfortable? Can you make sure they know exactly what to expect? Can they fill out their paperwork at home and bring it with them to save time? Have you given them confirmation calls with directions? Your clients want to get great results and will be fine once they get acclimated – make it as comfortable as you can for them to get started.*

Be The Total Solution – For us to go to a theme park like Disney World, it's not as simple as just showing up at the park. We have to worry about lodging, meals and travel. Disney has grown their business by allowing you to bundle all of it in together and stay at their hotels, eat at their restaurants and lean on them for travel. They even offer guides that can go with you around the parks, behind the scenes opportunities and even babysitters if parents want to go out for an evening.

Basically, anything that can potentially help you have the type of experience you want to have – they will provide (at a price).

***Your Ideal Business Takeaway:** Your clients want a certain result. Outside of workouts, what can you provide that will help them get that result? Supplements? Nutrition Coaching? A Kitchen Makeover? A Grocery Store Tour? Foam rollers? Personal equipment like their own bands or kettlebells? A percentage of your clients will want the upgrades and some will even want everything you have to offer.*

It's All About The Details – Disney is all about the details. Every resort, park area and attraction has a theme and the theme permeates throughout every aspect of that Disney experience. From the Cast Members' clothes to the décor – everything is detailed and consistent.

They also pay attention every detail from making the time spent waiting in lines tolerable to having photographers and 'photo spots' throughout the parks to make capturing memories easier.

Your Ideal Business Takeaway: What little things can you do to make your clients' experience better? Sweating the details will go a long way. Is your staff all speaking the 'same language' and on the same page? Is your facility clean? Are you giving your clients handouts and sending them personal cards to let them know they're valued? All the little things that you can do to help clients get results a little quicker and make their experience a little better will go a long way.

Keep Improving: Walt Disney called it 'plussing' – the act of continually improving something – and that's what Disney does. They're always evolving, from adding things like airline check-ins or Fast Passes to make things a little easier on guests to new marquee attractions and even new venues (what started as 1 park now encompasses 4 theme parks, two water parks and a shopping area). Even though we go yearly, there are still noticeable changes on each visit.

Your Ideal Business Takeaway: This should be a no brainer, but you should always be improving at your craft, at delivering the experience and at running your business. Don't just focus on the big things either. Every little improvement will separate you farther from the competition.

There are plenty of other lessons that both you and I can take away from Disney World that will help us improve our businesses, but we'll focus on these for now.

Now you may be wondering why I didn't talk specifically about money even though Disney makes a mint off of every guest. It's because without the experience & the details – the money isn't there. Without all of this Disney is just another theme park. But by focusing on delivering an extraordinary experience and sweating every detail Disney can charge a premium, they can have far more stores in their parks than they do attractions and they can get people to happily pay more to them than they would to any other vacation theme park.

So take these lessons and use them in your business. They've helped Disney build a global empire and can help you build a fitness empire of your own.

My Favorite Business Building Tip

One of my most memorable coaching calls came with a fitness pro who was seeking some specific advice on growing his business.

I gave him what I consider to be the best advice that I can give someone, but it comes with a disclaimer.

You see, this is also advice that I'm hesitant to give because it could potentially give someone the idea that they don't have to do the work, which obviously goes against everything that I teach.

So the advice that I gave him and that I'm going to give you now is this:

Determine your strengths – then build your business around them.

Let me back up for a minute.

The fitness entrepreneur I was talking with already ran a strong business and has enjoyed some success in his marketing efforts.

He told me that he knew that I was a fan of public speaking and networking, but he hadn't really done much with either of those marketing tactics. Instead of telling him that he needed to dive right into those two because they are two of the most powerful ways available to any fitness pro to grow their business, I surprised him and told him not to do either of them.

Did my thoughts about public speaking or networking change? Of course not.

But after talking with him a bit and discovering that he had some other real strengths that he could leverage to generate more clients – and which he would clearly enjoy more – it was obvious that the best solution for him wasn't going the networking and public speaking route.

He needed to play to his strengths.

So why is this scary for me to give this advice?

Given to the wrong person, it can be misconstrued as a free pass to be lazy.

This particular fitness entrepreneur has already used social media and his writing skills successfully to grow his business. Suggesting more ways for him to leverage his use of social media and his writing talents even more makes sense because he's already proven that it is successful for him.

However, put that same advice in the wrong hands, and you get a situation where someone who's never proven that they can write worth a darn and hasn't had any success with social media now thinks they don't have to ever get out from behind their computer to build a successful business.

In fact, back in the old Personal Trainer U days, there was a guy on the forum that did just that: he got on the forum and whined about how he'd written 3 articles and submitted them to article directories, put up a couple blog posts, and he didn't have any clients to show for it. The economy was to blame. There was no way that trainers could be successful right now.

My response was simple: "How many prospects are in your home office right now? If the answer is zero, then get off your butt and go where they are."

Needless to say, he didn't post anymore.

But that's my fear when dispensing this advice: people mistaking their strengths for what's just easiest.

But I've believed that this approach was the best way to go for quite a while.

When I was coaching baseball, it took me a couple years to quit trying to be a clone of the coach that I admired most. My strengths were different than his. Once I realized that, I became a much better coach, and our teams got much better.

I followed this same approach when it came to dealing with our opponents, too; instead of worrying about detailed scouting reports and trying to exploit opponents' weaknesses, I wanted our players to focus exclusively on playing to their strengths.

Heck, most any business success I've had was built on this approach and anytime I've hit a wall it's been when I've deviated from that.

Now, you may not think that this advice is anything special, but here's why it is:

Once you determine your strengths, by going all-in and leveraging them to the maximum, you've done 3 things:

1. You've separated yourself from everyone else because you're playing to your unique talents, assets, passions, and skills.

2. You just made running your business a lot more fun because you can focus more on doing what you're best at and feel confident that it's a good choice.

3. You just set out on the fastest route I know to build a powerhouse business.

Another way of putting this is, "Do more of what's working." Seems simple, right?

Well, most people don't do it. They jump from one thing they've had some success with to something else that requires completely different talents or skills instead of finding more ways to utilize the strengths that led to the successes they've had.

To use my business as an example, one of our strengths is connecting. Really, everything that I've built has been founded on building relationships with fitness professionals and trying to provide the best solutions they need to build the fitness business they want.

So once I recognized that connecting and creating relationships were at the core of my businesses, I started to do things like:

- Hold more live events to spend more time in person with the people we serve.
- Do more coaching calls so I can learn more about the people we work with and how we can most effectively help them.
- Make most of my business built around engagement based offerings…VFM, Courses, Masterminds and private consulting.

Those are just a few samples, but you get the picture.

So how can you leverage your strengths to build your business?

If you're a relationship person, do more connecting. Focus more on referrals. Create more thorough solutions for the people that you already work with. Build a community in your business so strong that it attracts the type of clients you want more of.

If you're great at writing, make sure you've got great copy on your site. Write like crazy. Write a column for the local paper. Build out email autoresponders. Send press releases. Send a great newsletter. Write free special reports that you can get in the hands of prospects. Write direct mail sequences to send out in your area.

And that's not even beginning to touch on how you can leverage your strengths as a coach to own a particular niche market.

So your goal should be this:

Figure out what your real strengths are – the things that you've proven that you're better than the rest at, the things you've done well to grow your business, the things that you not only enjoy doing but that produce results.

Once you've determined those strengths, figure out as many ways as you can to start leveraging them to build the business you want, and start implementing those ideas.

This philosophy will give you the resources to build a great business that you'll love owning.

2

Business Success

The 5 Rules of Lasting Fitness Business Success

All too often we spend our time on day to day things or working on the tactical level without spending much time on stepping back and working on our business.

The Five Rules of Lasting Business Success

Rule #1: Get Clear

Now, I used to think that 'getting clear' meant determining how many clients you wanted, how much revenue you planned to generate or even how much income you'd personally make. Those can be part of it…but they're not what I'm talking about in its entirety. The thing you need to get clear on is what success looks like to you…what your Ideal Business looks like. A subtle, but important distinction.

What does success look like to you? Do you know? Do you know what your Ideal Business looks like? What do you know want your life to look like? What is your professional mission?

You might think on the surface it's to make some money or own a fancy training facility. Often, we get tricked by ourselves to think that we're in this industry to make an okay living training clients…to serve others. But the reality is you want something more specific whether you have sat down and deliberately figured it out or not.

Here's mine...

Personally, I am very passionate about helping fellow fitness entrepreneurs build the business and the life that they want to have…while doing the same for myself. I talk on the phone to clients constantly working on this. I fly around the country for meetings and conferences to accomplish this…and I'm relentlessly studying to find better ways to accomplish this. This is my mission. This is Ideal for me.

There are two phases to this:

Phase I: What is your mission…what does the Ideal Business look like for you?

Here are some questions that might help you do this:

- What will you sacrifice to make it your reality?
- What is truly important to you personally and professionally?
- What is the outcome you're dedicated to?

For me, I'm willing to travel away from my family more than I want to in order to reach more fitness entrepreneurs or to learn better ways to serve them. It's important because I know a lot of wonderful professionals in our industry make some serious sacrifices to serve their clients. I think being able help the clients you want to and have the income, security and enough freedom to go on vacation or coach your kid's Little League team shouldn't be mutually exclusive.

It's something that I've experienced from both sides – as the burned out coach, putting in ridiculous hours for low pay and no retirement…and as the fitness entrepreneur who can have a significant impact on the people I want to help while still enjoying a family friendly lifestyle and an income that matches the impact I have.

People are going to doubt you…they're going to try to kill your dreams. You're going to try things and they won't succeed like you planned. What's going to keep you going? It's that Mission…it's your Ideal Business and all that it yields. So get clear on it! When you're clear on where you're going, lots of other things just fall into place automatically.

Phase II: Why is it so important?

My mission is important to me because I feel that 98% of fitness entrepreneurs settle in life. They settle for less than they are capable of…less than they deserve.

They get up early every day, hustle into the gym, help dozens…even hundreds of *other* people reach their goals…enjoy a better, healthier, more fulfilling life…all while barely making ends meet, sacrificing time with their family, failing to save money for the future, accepting that a large percentage of the people they train will be people they don't enjoy simply because they have to pay the bills, rarely – if ever – taking a vacation, not having time for their family or their own personal interests…all this on the path to burnout or exhaustion. Their only solace is that they get to have their own training business…even if it doesn't at all resemble what they originally set out to build.

It's important because I don't want that for you and won't accept that for myself. So that's my "why" and I can't stand idly by and have the knowledge of how to overcome that and not share it with fellow trainers and coaches.

It's important to understand your "why" as you think about what you want your Mission and your Ideal Business to look like…and my 'whys' are my family and to help other entrepreneurs.

The clarity that you have when you discover where you want to go and the "why" behind it – you'll gain the conviction and the drive to do all that is necessary for lasting success. Because I can assure you, lasting business success takes a tremendous amount of work but if you're clear on where you're going, it doesn't feel like work at all. Writing the newsletters I write…coaching the fitness entrepreneurs I work with…they don't feel much like work at all.

Now I'm not saying that some of what you do won't feel like work because it will. But if you have clarity of purpose, clarity of mission, clarity of what success looks like to you…then you'll be excited about what you are doing because you'll know that it's moving you toward where you want to go and you'll know what sort of impact you're having each and every day.

One more point...

You also need to get clear to what you should be doing. For me the 3 things I should be doing...the things I'm best at and most passionate about are creating, coaching and 'ideation'.

Creating opportunities, resources, relationships and content.

Coaching...be it fitness entrepreneurs or baseball players.

And Ideation...developing ideas or recognizing opportunities, either for my own business or for others.

And the higher percentage of my time I invest in those things and the more of the things that fall outside of those areas that I outsource to people whose strengths complement mine...the faster I move toward my Ideal Business and the happier I am. So, in addition to getting clear about what success looks like to you and what your personal mission is, you also need to get clear about what you personally should be doing.

Rule #2: Work

One of the biggest misconceptions about the concept of building your Ideal Business is that it doesn't require work, wrong. Anything worth having requires work, no exceptions. But most people...even most business owners...don't do strategic work that will move them to their goals. They substitute busy work…and no one ever achieved any great success by spending most of their time on busy work.

If you read this and then just sit around and reflect on what you learned without doing anything, you'll actually lose ground and be farther from your goals because you'll have wasted your time.

We all already know things we could take strategic action on and here's why it's so important in the bigger picture of achieving success. When you do strategic work you have confidence. Action breeds more action. You feel good about yourself and your ability to achieve success.

If you want to feel unstoppable, do something that moves you toward your goals. Play to your strengths and do something specific that moves you toward the business you want. Do it and see what happens. Measure the results. Do it every day.

If not for the immediate results, do it for what happens in your mind when you do it because you go from thinking to doing. You're making progress…no matter how small. Your identity becomes someone who does and it becomes routine. Once it becomes routine, it leads to expansion for more action. And, the only way to achieve lasting success is constant action.

You have more potential that you can probably imagine, but unless that potential is fed by the best beliefs, attitudes, and resources… then followed up by consistent action, it remains untapped.

Tony Robbins has a Success Cycle that I think is spot on:

Potential > Action > Results > Beliefs

What happens is you have this potential, and based on that, you take action. Based on the action you take you produce results. Then, based on the results you get, this feeds your beliefs about what you think your potential is. You can impact this cycle positively at any point.

If you feed your mind with new beliefs, you activate your potential for greater results. When you put that potential to the test by taking new actions, you'll get more and better results. This turns into more positive beliefs and attitudes you hold about yourself and your ability to succeed. These new beliefs and attitudes will unleash even more of your potential, leading to better actions, better results, and on and on. This spiral of success builds incredible momentum.

So if you start taking action, you'll start to get results and this will feed the whole cycle. When you take action, it gives you confidence so when you're confronted with failure or negativity, you can withstand it and not get derailed.

So focus on investing time in work daily that moves you toward your goals…toward your Ideal Business. Plan your day the evening prior and schedule time to work on building the business that you want. If you can schedule time for others, then you can certainly schedule time for you. Start doing at least a little of this work daily and you'll create momentum that will make you virtually unstoppable.

Rule #3: Embrace Simplicity

If you want to achieve your goals and have lasting business success, then you need to simplify things. If you try to make things too complicated, you won't execute them and others won't be able to follow your plan. In fact, if things are too complicated it leads to overwhelm and paralysis. Sure, you need to make educated decisions…but you can't let the burden of too much, too much information or too much on your task list, slow you down.

As an entrepreneur you have an advantage, if you choose to use it…you are relatively little and can act quickly. You can move much more quickly than bigger, more bureaucratic businesses…but it's up to you.

As a small business owner trying to affect positive change, there's a lot going on. You can't have clutter. You have a choice…you can be overwhelmed and struggle to get your massive list of things done or you can do a few things and be extraordinary at them.

Imagine an airline pilot with all the stuff he's doing also trying to keep track of the latest gizmo or shiny object. He'd crash the plane with all 700 people on it. The drivers in your business are important. Everything matters. So you need to simplify.

In fact, I try to simplify business as much as I can…so here's how I look at business in a very simplistic, 3 step way:

Step 1 - Lead Generation
Step 2 - Conversion
Step 3 - Delivery

Sure – each of those are comprised of various parts, but to keep things simple you can ask yourself each day:

Did you generate leads?

Did you sell?

Did you fulfill or deliver on your promise?

If you lose focus and become distracted by overwhelm…you're not the best version of you in any way. So simplify.

Here's another part of simplification and one that's going to sound strange coming from me. Clear out the information overload. You can't study a dozen different 'experts' in business and a dozen in training and actually execute. Pick a couple, learn from them and apply. The others get put on hold for a while. Ignore them. Put them into a folder…or (gasp) unsubscribe. Focus on execution instead of simply gathering information.

Identify your mission – what success looks like to you - and come up with a plan. Then you have to commit to that plan. You can refine the plan or update it or better yet – simplify it. Then it's time to focus on execution.

Simplicity leads to Clarity. Clarity leads to the ability to take rapid, decisive Action. Anything else will slow or even kill your progress. Keep it simple and take massive action.

Rule #4: Be Bold

Most people lead average lives…because they aren't bold. To achieve anything extraordinary you have to be bold. You have to be willing to get a little uncomfortable and challenge the norms.

Back in my baseball coaching days I spent my first two seasons playing it safe, doing things the way that everyone else did them and the results were pretty average. But when I was willing to challenge conventional wisdom and approach things differently, that's when we became a Championship program.

Then, to achieve success in my first business, Holly, Tyler & I lived in a basement for a year. This wasn't in my early twenties…I was 33. Something that most others would be unwilling to do. A bold choice.

I could have stayed in coaching baseball. I had job offers at both the collegiate and the professional level, but while that would have been the comfortable option, it wasn't going to get me to the success I was looking for.

And I had a few job opportunities in sales that were certainly 'safer' and more secure. Jobs that would have been more financially rewarding at the time. But again that wasn't my dream, my mission.

To do anything big, you've got to be bold.

Most recently, moving on from an organization I'd been building for a decade to pursue my Ideal Business and start focusing on a few things that no one else was teaching (and many thought were not possible)—helping you create your Ideal Business…again, it was bold. But with no risk comes no reward.

And you're going to screw things up. You're going to make people mad. You're going to fail. I've done all three more times than I can remember. I've had so many fails that it's nothing more than a bump in the road when it happens now, it's just part of the process.

Professionally, I look back and my first and biggest 'fail' was being forced to resign after a 4-year battle with a Vice President of the

University where I coached. I'd built a successful program with some really, really meager resources and being the baseball coach was my entire identity. Resigning, or essentially being fired, was crushing. My self-esteem was at an all-time low. But instead of playing it safe and avoiding risks, in an attempt to avoid feeling like a failure again, I took even bolder steps moving forward, recognizing the pain associated with my first big fail was just a knockdown from which I could dust myself off and get back up. Oh…and 10 years later that same University held a baseball tournament named after me and also named me the University's Distinguished Alumnus.

Failure is only a bump in the road. It's a test to weed out the uncommitted. Be bold. It's in the moments when you get back up that your fortune is made. That your goals are realized. You will have challenges, struggles and failures. Just deal with it. Accept it. In fact, welcome it and know that overcoming it will separate you from those who are average.

Now, the formula that allows you to do this really goes back to the first step when we clarified what success looks like to you. Because when you have a mission that's truly meaningful to you, that's the only thing that will pull you through all of the inevitable obstacles you're going to encounter along the way. I can assure you, the rewards of being bold outweigh any benefit of playing small. When you're crystal clear, everything else unfolds. You get the willingness, the drive to take action, the ability to make the right decisions and you're able to get past the obstacles in the way.

#5: Everything Matters

What I mean by this is that every single choice or action are either moving us closer to or farther from our goals. We're a product of our choices. Our businesses and our lives are reflections of the actions we did or didn't take.

Are your clients getting the results they should be getting? If not, it's almost always a reflection of the choices they're making. Eating things that aren't congruent with getting results. Too many drinks on the weekend. Not enough sleep.

The same is every bit as true with us and our goals. Every day we have the option to plan tomorrow or to simply wake up and react to what comes our way. Every day we choose how we're feeding our mind…what we're reading or learning from. Every day we decide how we're going to engage (or fail to engage) with the people in our lives…from our family and friends to our clients and prospects. We decide if we're going to take specific actions to move toward our goals or put them off until tomorrow.

In truth – we decide whether we believe success is even possible. Our self-talk is often the first domino for many of the choices we'll make.

We decide who we spend our time with…and I'll tell you that if you spend your time with negative people…you're going to be negative. If you surround yourself with others who play small…so will you.

And you don't really get to pick and choose which decisions actually matter. Which choices will be important. You never know how you treat someone on a given day will impact you, your relationship or even your business a year down the road. You never know when the seminar you attend or the book you read will be the one that changes everything.

I've seen people's lives ruined...or even ended...by a poor choice. I've seen people's lives forever improved by a single, seemingly simple choice too. It's a powerful reminder that every little thing we choose affects us. Sometimes we just become so numb to it, we don't realize how powerful of an effect it's really having on us and how we're moving toward or away from our goals. Every single thing matters.

So there are **The 5 Rules of Lasting Business Success:**

Rule #1: Get Clear
Rule #2: Work
Rule #3: Embrace Simplicity
Rule #4: Be Bold
Rule #5: Everything Matters

They're not tactical. They're not magic bullets or quick fixes. They're the foundation that any success you want to have can and will be built on. Embrace them and virtually any goal you set out to achieve will ultimately be yours.

3 Lessons

There are only 3 things that my business is built on...and they've always been at the core of any professional success I've had.

1. Play To Your Strengths: I have touched on this a lot...because it's what I feel we should all do.

Dan Sullivan (a guy far smarter than me) calls it Unique Ability and we all have it.

We all have a few things that we're good at...and my belief is that we should spend as much of our time on that stuff as we can and let people whose strengths are different than ours do the stuff that's not in our wheelhouse.

I'm only good at a few things...and the higher percentage of my time I spend on those things...the better my business is.

2. Keep It Simple: I feel like most people over-complicate things. I want to take the simplest path to the destination.

I'd rather have a simple business model and try to be great at a few things than a complex one that requires me to try (and often struggle) at a bunch of stuff.

3. Recognizing Opportunities: Most of the things I've had success with professionally have been the result of recognizing opportunities that others didn't see or others didn't value.

Opportunities to transplant ideas from other industries.
Opportunities to leverage my strengths and assets.
Opportunities to do things a bit differently.

Opportunities are all around us...but you have to look for them. If you wait around for the obvious ones you'll be late to the party.

That's it.

And while the stuff that drives my business isn't rocket science or some lengthy list...I'm proud of it. I think the path to each of our own Ideal Businesses is shorter and easier to navigate than most people would guess...and the simplicity of what I do just reinforces that.

So if things aren't where you want them or you aren't moving as fast as you'd like to where you want to be...use this list as a guide and I'm guessing you'll start progressing much, much faster.

Focus on These Success Keys

Recently, I was working on a copywriting project for a colleague and I started to give some thought to how important something like that is to a business.

He could have the best product on the planet, but if the copy doesn't reflect that...well, no one might ever know.

But I think why I like copywriting so much is that it provides leverage.

You write one compelling sales message and it can essentially be your automated sales person to thousands.

And good sales copy can be a game changer.

A few years back someone suggested I delegate writing sales copy - so I explained the numbers to them.

Let's say that for a product, my sales page converts at 5% to the audience it's in front of (that's a high percentage for cold traffic, but very manageable when in front of an audience who already knows, likes and trusts you).

And let's say that if I'd have delegated it...and the junior copywriter's page converted at 3%.

If each page was selling a $100 product and each page got 20,000 clicks - mine generated $100,000 and his generated $60,000.

A difference like that could be the difference between profitability and losing money if you're running ads. Between business failure and success depending on what your overhead is.

Regardless...the difference is a LOT of money.

That's the power of a leverage point.

There are a few real leverage points that you have at your disposal if you want to use them...here are a few:

Good Sales Copy - I just shared how that can provide you some powerful leverage.

A Responsive Email List - Once you have a responsive email list, you can send one message and it's seen by hundreds or even thousands. One of the 2 most powerful leverage points I think you can have.

Training Multiple People At Once - Here you're leveraging your time and skill - it's become common in the industry today, but for a long time this simple leverage point wasn't appreciated.

Systems - With these in place you can scale your business and leverage your knowledge so that it's used to allow others to execute on your behalf.

Skill Development - If you get better at selling, the same time invested will yield more sales. Get better at program design and you can take less time to write the same or better programs.

Online Products & Programs - Through this channel you can scale your business beyond your local area and share what works for you globally.

Borrowed Expertise - I think this may be the most powerful leverage point of all. When someone comes to do a 1-day consulting session with me, they're essentially getting a decade of my knowledge and experience in a day. All my trial and error, everything I've done and gone through - distilled down and shared with them in a way that is specific to their business.

Any sort of continuing education works that way to a degree. From books to conferences...you're leveraging someone else's knowledge and experience.

There are plenty of others - but these are my favorites. The most important thing is that you look for ways to create leverage in your business and your life. You'll get where you're trying to go much, much faster.

How to Be #1

One of the more insightful thoughts on becoming #1 in your market comes from someone outside the fitness industry.

The man who was widely regarded as the best CEO of the last 50 years, Jack Welch, set a goal when he took over General Electric…

…to be #1 or #2 in any category GE was in. If they couldn't be #1 or #2, he wanted to get out of that business.

Now obviously, we're not dealing with corporate giants…but I think the same mindset still applies.

You need to be #1 or #2 in your market for what you do…and if you aren't you either need to get better or redefine what it is that you do.

So how do you get to that 1st or 2nd spot:

Be First - If you are the first person in a market that does or offers a particular thing…you have a big advantage. My friend John Spencer Ellis founded Adventure Bootcamp years ago and a lot of his licensees had incredible success right out of the gate, in part because they were the first bootcamp in their market.

If you think about people who make a lot of money in small towns…it's often people who take business concepts they see in bigger cities and transplant them to the smaller towns. The first person who brought a popular fast food restaurant to a small town usually did pretty well for themselves.

Be Better - There is always room at the top. If you're great at what you do - you can succeed...as long as people know about it. The goal is for you to never be referred to as a 'hidden gem'.

If you have the best service, deliver the best results and create the best experience...you can thrive no matter if you're first or last to market...as long as you expose people to it.

Be Different - This is my favorite way to capture that #1 spot...Be Different.

See, being different means that you have built on some market awareness...so there is already a demand for something that is generally in your market.

But by putting a new twist on it, by doing some things differently, being perceived differently, by blending in some new elements, you've actually become first in a new category and are the best in that category (because you're now basically one of a kind).

What's great about these 3 ways to compete and win is that they work for your business as a whole...but they work for components of your business too.

So if you are first to use a new marketing channel or if you market differently than everyone else...the same benefits apply.

So here's a simple exercise for you to use this information:

Think about you and your competition...then answer the following:

Were you first to market? If not, who was?

Are you better than them? If so, how (be specific)? Are you better in marketing? Service? Experience? How? If not...how can you get there?

Are you different? Different in the public's eye...not just your opinion? How?

Put your business under the microscope.

Make sure you're setting yourself up to be in that #1 or #2 position and to enjoy long term success.

Answer This or Fail

"Why should the prospects that you want choose you over all the other options they have available to them?"

If you can't answer that...your business will never be more than average.

And don't tell me it's because you have a specific certification or credential.

You care about that a lot more than they do.

Think about it from the other side...the side of being the consumer.

The last time you had a great steak, had you chosen the restaurant by where the chef went to culinary school?

Did you choose your family doctor or dentist by their medical or dental school?

Didn't think so.

So don't expect people to choose you by that criteria either.

So if that's not it…what will they use as their criteria?

Well, first and foremost…convenience. If you are in L.A. and the prospect is in Boston…they won't be stopping by your facility very often.

But after that?

Can you solve the problem they want solved?

Remember…it's about them. If they want 'fat loss' and you sell 'move better' they're not choosing you.

Then, are you credible?

Can they trust that you can solve their problem? That's why referrals are so powerful…instant credibility.

Social proof.

Endorsements and media credits.

Credentials.

All part of being credible about solving the problem they want solved.

Then finally, are they comfortable?

Are they comfortable with you? Do they like you and your team?

Are they comfortable with the culture? The experience? The style?

Are they comfortable with the investment?

They've got to be comfortable to choose you.

Bring all those answers together and now you can convey…

"Why should the prospects that you want choose you over all the other options they have available to them?"

Fail to answer this and you're destined for a mediocre business, but get it right and marketing will become the easiest thing you do.

Continuous Improvement

I'm a lifelong Cincinnati Reds fan and we regularly attend games.

One of my favorite things about the Reds games is how the stadium and the fan experience has evolved and improved over time.

I remember going to games at old Riverfront Stadium when I was younger and the fan experience was a complete afterthought (if not ignored all together).

Now, it's great…even if you're not a baseball fan they've constructed an experience that will allow you to really enjoy yourself.

And since a new ownership group took over a few years ago, every new season equals a number of improvements to the overall experience.

Now, neither of our businesses is anything like theirs. I get that for sure. And I think that for the most part, what works for big business doesn't usually translate very well to our small operations.

But they're in the experience business and so are we.

And for both them and us, the status quo is never good enough.

We each have to continue to improve.

There is always something new competing for the people we want to serve's attention and for us to win new people or hang on to our current ones – we've got to continually improve what we offer.

So what are you doing to improve your client experience?

What could you tweak that would be more appealing to your best clients?

I know that in my case, one thing that I'm doing is giving the Virtual Fitness Mastermind a makeover.

I didn't like the platform we used, so I'm changing to something new and more user-friendly.

I'm hoping to have this ready to go next week…but after that's done I'm sure I'll be working on improving something else.

I know that to build *my* Ideal Business I'm going to have to continually improve things until the programs, products and courses that I offer are not only the most effective at helping you build *your* Ideal Business, but they need to also be the easiest to use and simplest to put into action.

In your world it's pretty much the same.

You're not only going to have to be the best at delivering results for the clients you serve, but you also need to create the best culture in your facility and community with your clients.

My suggestion to you to help make this happen is 'model success.'

If there is something you like about a business you frequent – see how you can model what they do in your own business.

Then put it into action.

Alright, I'll wrap it up here because 'put it into action' is about the best place to wrap up most of the time.

The Difference Maker

More than anything else, coaching is your difference maker.

It's not equipment – anyone can go and stock a facility with equipment.

And in spite of what many want to believe – it's not knowledge either. Sure, that matters…without a doubt. Your clients won't know what you know…but the information is available to your clients that if they want enough knowledge to yield the results they want…they can get it.

No, the one thing that big box clubs stuffed with equipment won't ever match you in…the one area that buying info products and books can't ever compete…is coaching.

You can bring out the best in people.

You can help them achieve things they would never do on their own.

Accountability.

Motivation.

Problem solving.

Personal attention.

These are things that 99% of the fitness solutions out there will never provide.

Yes, 99%. That number seems high doesn't it?

It's high because most fitness professionals settle for hosting workouts and passing along information. They've settled for being little more than the group exercise class at the local YMCA.

But the shortcomings of most is your gain if you want it to be.

You can be that person who helps people become the best version of themselves.

You can be the person who coaches someone to unlock their true potential...potential that they likely didn't even realize they had.

You just have to be willing to do what most won't do...truly coach.

I've been coaching since 1993 (yes, it's been a while) and I've studied countless things to get better...I've read books on leadership and biographies of great coaches. I've attended seminars and conferences. But my favorite way to become better as a coach is to learn directly from another successful coach.

That's why I'm currently going through the Training For Warriors Certification.

While the goals my clients have these days are different than the goals your clients have in most cases, coaching is still coaching. And after watching Martin Rooney present any number of times at Perform Better, I knew he was a coach I could learn from.

The Truth About Hard Work

Growing up, hard work was a badge of honor.

"That guy is a hard worker."

It was the strongest compliment a lot of people could give.

If someone was willing to sweat a little more or go a little longer...they were deemed successful.

But I'll tell you what I figured out about that over the years...it's a pretty dumb way of looking at things.

I grew up working in my dad's garage...first as a janitor and later as a janitor / mechanic during the summers.

I can't count how many times I was under the hood of a car, sweating (during the summers it felt like an oven in there) and straining like crazy trying to get a part loose only to have my dad come over with a different tool and have it loose in less than a minute.

Smart work beats hard work.

Then, as a baseball coach I remember how I spent my time versus how the coach that followed me in the same position spent his.

I focused about 90% of my time of recruiting players and developing players.

We won about 70% of our games.

He focused about 20% of his time on those things…instead spending more time just hanging out at the field. The field was prettier under his watch but he won about 45% of his games.

Now make no mistake…I've yet to meet a person who didn't put in a lot of hours working hard that achieved any degree of success.

I've never met someone who built a great business using a four-hour workweek.

But then again…I've never met someone who's built a great business that they actually enjoy who simply worked hard without working smart.

So how can you start working smart…well, here are a few thoughts to help you:

- Decide where you want to go and develop a plan to get there. Then work the plan.
- Understand that being busy is not a point of price. Anyone can be busy…the better question is 'who gets more of the right stuff done each day?'
- Go into your day with the Most Important Tasks…2-3 at most. Do those before doing anything else.
- When you spend time on something you're actually saying 'this is the most valuable thing I could be doing right now.' Think about your activities that way and look for ways to spend less time doing the things you decide aren't really that valuable.

I think Abraham Lincoln summed up the way I feel about this very well:

"Give me six hours to chop down a tree and I will spend the first four sharpening the axe."

He didn't suggest to shy away from the six hours of work…he simply suggested using that six hours more wisely that most would.

That's how you get better results than the rest.

The 5 Letter Key to Success

F.O.C.U.S.

Most people do too much.

Their businesses and their lives are cluttered with unnecessary activities, busy work and an array of 'crap' that prevents them from doing what is important.

They waste their most valuable commodity – time – responding to the perceived urgent while ignoring the truly important.

They're super busy…but they're not nearly as effective as they could and should be.

Activity wins over achievement almost every day.

The most successful people narrow their Focus and spend their time on the things that will give them the business and the life that they want…and they delegate, eliminate, minimize or systemize the rest.

If you want to have your Ideal Business, you have to spend time with the most important people and doing the most important tasks.

You have to be productive…not just busy.

Greatness never comes by accident.

You have goals. FOCUS on them and go get them.

Learning from The Final Four [Game Changer]

A few years back, my good friend Chris Simmons got me 4 All-Access passes for the Final Four. Holly and I went with our good friends Jeff and Lara and it was a great time.

But, in addition to it being a fun event and a great time hanging out with friends, it was also a reminder of how we can draw business lessons from sport.

For the purposes of this lesson, I'm just going to focus on college basketball for a moment. While Duke won the National Championship, each of the teams that got to the Final Four had great teams and each played their own unique style of basketball.

It's just like business.

There are a number of different approaches to getting client results…you've got your own style just like those programs and the coaches who lead them do.

But here's where things get really obvious…recruiting.

See, it's no coincidence that the best teams have the best players.

Not only can all of those coaches recruit (i.e. - sell), but they all sell the unique benefits of their program.

They'll each sell how their system can make the recruits better players, will give them the best chance to win, will provide them the best education and (one of the biggest selling points) will get them to the NBA.

Each has their own unique spin…their own unique angle.

And each succeeds.

Make no mistake…this is the lifeblood of their winning programs. Not the tactical stuff.

Even the best tactical coaches won't win very often with bad players.

It's so much like what we do, it's scary.

You've got your own unique approach to delivering results…but if you can't compel people to be part of your programs, your business will fail.

Sure - you can get clients that aren't exactly who you'd consider ideal if you drop prices and sound like everyone else…just like coaches who are poor recruiters can fill out a roster with mediocre players…but you can't succeed over time with that approach.

There are countless other similarities between sports and business…folks much smarter and more successful than me draw the comparisons all the time. However, the recruiting one is something most miss, but it rings true with me after years recruiting as a coach myself.

So, I'll close by giving you the recruiting formula that worked for me and actually caused one publication to refer to me as The Best Small College Recruiter in the Country…

1. Have a Program that Doesn't Blend In. Build it to appeal to the things that your ideal prospects want.

2. Sell Your Strengths and Downplay Your Shortcomings. Focus on the things you're better at than everyone else.

3. Be Congruent. Make sure every part of your recruiting pitch reflects what makes you uniquely appealing.

4. Know Your Perfect Prospect. Identify the people who will be the best fit for your program and know where to find them.

5. Recruit Relentlessly. Go after your best prospects hard and make sure they know that they're important to you.

6. Recruiting Is Never Ending. Once they commit, keep recruiting them. Your most important recruits are the ones who are already part of your program.

That approach allowed me to recruit successfully and if you apply it in your business it will allow you to do the same.

Put it to work.

P.S. - I'm going to let you in on a little secret…I try to teach you a handful of concepts using a variety of different methods…comparing business to sports is an example of that. But I'll take it a step further…the two concepts that trump all else are that you need to deliver a great solution (the training and the experience that goes with it) and you need to be able to pull the right clients into that service.

Those two things are 1A and 1B. Everything else revolves around those two. You'll be told and sold a bazillion different things as a business owner, but anyone telling you those aren't 1A and 1B is either mistaken or foolish. It's too easy to get pulled into focusing on a bunch of low ROI things, so keep those at the top of your priority list and you'll be headed in the right direction.

The Power of 1%

One of the biggest differentiators between a great business and an average one is that the great one keeps improving. They keep evolving their business and making it 1% better, over and over.

Someone who looks at a great business's sales or assessment system may say "that doesn't look that different from what I do." But again – the great ones keep improving things, 1% at a time.

And if you look at their businesses, all the things that they do from their Success Session to their Referral Systems to their Training Systems don't necessarily look like something you've never seen before…they just do them all a little bit better than most everyone else. That's why the best businesses succeed…they take what works, they plug it into their business and they 'plus it' over and over…improving each component by 1% time and time again.

And when it's all said and done you have a business that has maybe 20 different components which are each 10-20% better (at minimum) than the competition. But because of the compound effect, this doesn't make their business 10-20% better. Because every piece works synergistically with the others their improvement actually multiplies the improvement of the other areas. It's the difference between 100 clients and 400. The difference between $150,000 a year and $750,000.

If that seems hard to believe, here's how a 20% increase compounded changes things, illustrated another way:

- 10 X 10 x 10 x 10 x 10 x 10 x 10 x 10 x 10 x 10 = 10,000,000,000

- 12 x 12 x 12 x 12 x 12 x 12 x 12 x 12 x 12 x 12 = 61,917,364,224

12 is only 20% bigger than 10, but compounded the difference is HUGE.

So how can you put this into action?

Model Success

That's what you're doing by reading this, so you're already off to a good start. The best business owners I know may have invented a few things from scratch, but most of the components of their businesses were things that they learned from other successful fitness pros and businesses that they adapted, improved and made their own. So study what's working. Borrow from successful businesses. Model their success.

Implement

We all see dozens of good ideas…in products, at events, in Mastermind Meetings. But I'd guess most people actually implement about 2% of what they learn. The best businesses are living, breathing pictures of implementation. All the things people say they're going to implement – the best ones actually do.

Remember – it's not what you know. It's what you do. You can say you're a relationship business, but if you drop the ball over and over

– you're not. You can say you're all about referrals, but if you don't have referral systems in place that are working – you're not. The best implement. So should you.

Plussing

'Plussing' is a Walt Disney term for continually improving and it should be a regular part of your vocabulary. You may learn a referral system from someone and implement it, but you shouldn't settle for it 'as is.' You should always be looking for ways to make it a little more effective. We often talk about getting 1% better. This is getting 1% better in action.

Improving your referral reward or the way you ask. Improving your internal language. Improving your training system. 1% at a time. This 'plussing' will eventually give you that 10-20% edge in every area that the best business owners have.

So that's it. Your 'all too simple' way to build a powerhouse business. Put it into action and reap the same rewards that the industry's best businesses have reaped.

Get Started Today, 1% At A Time.

The 10X Approach

Building your Ideal Business isn't easy. How do you separate yourself from the competition? How do you rise above the countless options available to the market? Well, if you're looking for the easy route – there isn't one, but there is a simple and direct approach.

The 10X Approach.

It's not some magic bullet…but it will almost assuredly guarantee your success and success isn't easy. But you shouldn't want it to be easy. You shouldn't want everyone to be able to do it. That just makes it ordinary. Average. And I don't want to settle for any part of being average – and neither should you.

So here's the **10X Approach**…

1. You must commit to delivering 10 times the fee in the value you provide for anything you sell.

2. You must be willing to work 10 times harder and smarter than your competition.

3. You must be willing to set written goals 10 times loftier than you ever have before.

4. You must commit to being 10 times more knowledgeable than the competition.

5. You must get 10 times more done than the competition.

I know, that sounds challenging, right? It's supposed to. If you want to accomplish something that most people never will, you've got to be willing to do things that most people would never even consider doing.

The **first** principle is the foundation of the **10X Approach**:

You must commit to delivering 10 times the fee in the value you provide for anything you sell.

If you charge $199 a month for training, then you have to do your best to deliver $1990 in monthly value. I know that most people wouldn't pay you $1990 a month. Most people probably couldn't even if they wanted to and that's not the point.

The point is that you relentlessly work to deliver $10 in value for every $1 you charge. You give more personal attention to your people than anyone else does. You constantly strive to make your workouts more effective and more fun. You send cards on birthdays and you give gifts at Christmas. You give clients workouts they can take when they travel, and you give them guides or coaching on using anything you sell them.

If you spend some time every day looking for ways to deliver just a little more value, to make the experience that you provide just a little better, then you'll get to that point where you achieve **#1**. And you know that the competition isn't doing this. They're trying to figure out how little they can get away with giving for the fee they charge. But remember: people either want the cheapest or they want the best, and this is how you become the best.

The **second** component of the **10X Approach** is simple, but it will weed out 99% of the people who ever own a business:

You must be willing to work 10 times harder and smarter than your competition.

If you embrace this, it's a competitive advantage that the others in your market won't step up to match. I didn't say that you have to work longer – just harder and smarter.

When your competition is searching online, trying to find ways to avoid work, you work. When they think they know enough, you study. You're either getting better or worse – every day. Spend most or all of your days getting better.

In spite of what some "experts" will tell you, there is no instant path to success. Heck, even if you win the lottery, you had to get off your butt and go buy a ticket. Take pride in outworking people. The leaders in nearly any field know more about how to be successful than their competition and they work harder. You can do the same. It's a decision.

The **third** component of the **10X Approach** is one that every mediocre business owner ignores:

You must be willing to set written goals 10 times loftier than you ever have before.

Most business owners make every day like the movie *Groundhog Day*. They get up and do the same thing over and over. They have no real goals that drive them forward. If you're building your Ideal Business, you can't make this critical mistake. Why settle for mediocrity? Why be comfortable with being average?

John F. Kennedy said, *"Once you say you're going to settle for second, that's what happens to you in life."*

So if you're going to build a business, why settle for anything less than great? Building a business is hard work. I've been there. I remember not having enough money to fill up my gas tank when we were getting started. I remember having to go on Craigslist to try to find discounted tickets to be able to take Tyler to a local amusement park because we couldn't afford them at full price. Nevertheless, having lofty goals was the carrot out in front that kept me motivated, and it keeps me striving to learn and get better every day. Most people won't set those types of goals. You must.

Component **#4** is something I see with my private clients and Masterminders all the time:

You must commit to being 10 times more knowledgeable than the competition.

The best don't get there by accident. I look at some of my clients and I'm amazed by how much they know. They already know how to get people amazing results, and still they're the first ones to keep studying. They know more about business than the rest of the industry, but they are the first to dive in and keep improving. Being the best means always staying one step ahead, and part of that is being a lifelong learner.

The **final** component of the **10X Approach** is simply:

You must get 10 times more done than the competition.

Because, ultimately, no one cares what you know, how much potential you have, or how smart and talented you are. They don't care about all your good ideas or the countless projects you start.

They sure as hell don't care about the promises you make. They care about what you do and what you accomplish.

So if you're building your Ideal Business – one that provides a great experience for all that come in contact with it and personal satisfaction, wealth, and freedom for you – don't focus on activity. Focus on achievement.

Remember: You only get paid for done.

So are you up to the task? Are you one of the rare fitness professionals that wants to be great and wants to build your Ideal Business that is in that top 1% of all in our field? If so - start with the **10X Approach**.

The X Factor for Business Success

If you really want to know the thing that allows some people to enjoy success while others settle for mediocrity – it's really pretty simple.

Drive.

If one of your clients wants to reach their goals, it's more about their want, desire and willingness to stick to your program than it is about having any magic system.

If you want to build your Ideal Business, it's more about your hunger and willingness to do what most won't than it is about the latest greatest marketing fad or business system.

The truth is – a lot of different approaches will work…

…If you will.

I can look back and see this clearly hold true in pretty much any success I've ever had and for all the successful people I've known.

When I became a Baseball Coach, the two previous coaches at that University had been a former Major League All-Star and a legendary high school coach that had made the jump to coaching at the collegiate level.

Both struggled in the job I was about to take – and both had tons more experience, credentials and resources.

I was 23 and I can look back and count on one hand the number of people that expected me to be even modestly successful – and that's including myself.

But the fear of failure drove me tirelessly. With less experience, worse facilities and poorer resources than virtually everyone we competed against – I was able to be successful because I was willing to do what others wouldn't.

When other coaches we're vacationing during the summer, I was working.

When they were home, I was recruiting.

While they were comfortable, I was hungry.

Really, I was just unwilling to fail and it drove me constantly.

When I moved into the business world, I'd only read 4 books that could be considered 'business books' in my life, I'd never made more than $33,000 in a year and I'm pretty sure I was about as unprepared for success as someone could be.

But after taking about 18 months to work for someone for a while to learn the ropes of the industry and study up on business – I took the leap into entrepreneurship and went into business. But this time that Drive - and that fear of failure - was even bigger.

At that point, everyone I'd known in my life thought of me as a baseball coach and always expected me to go back to that. So that fear of failure gnawed at me again. But there was a second Driver that wouldn't let me fail. Family.

When we got started, Holly, Tyler and I lived in a basement for a year and under no circumstances was I going to fail them. Everyone has their stories like this where they struggled and paid their dues.

It's just that most of them aren't in their early thirties – but that was a choice I'd made since I'd decided to change careers mid-stream. And as far as I was concerned, failure was not an option.

Looking back, in both cases I had a lot fewer resources and experience than the competition. But that was made up for with Drive.

But this Drive – or willingness to do what others won't is hardly exclusive to me. I know plenty of people who exhibit it more than I do or ever have.

I've been fortunate enough to work with a LOT of successful entrepreneurs and they all use different business models, different marketing strategies and even different training methods in one way or another.

But the one thing you'll find in all of them – and every other successful person – is Drive.

The Contrarian Fitness Business

I want to give you a great tip I picked up at the Dan Kennedy Super Conference from Dan Kennedy himself.

He said, "Most times you can jump to the top of any industry simply by doing everything the opposite of your competition."

I think back to launching our personal training business and only selling training in 30 minute sessions and on 12 month contracts when everyone else did hour sessions and short term packages.

Starbucks approached selling coffee from as opposite a perspective as could be.

Southwest airlines focused on getting people from one place to another on time for a low price – something unheard of in the airline industry.

If you want to be successful, look at what all the other trainers and clubs are doing – then do the opposite. If they're all selling 1 hour, one-on-one sessions, then you should do 30 minute sessions, small group training or bootcamps.

They sell in 12 and 24 packs.

You do 6 and 12 month agreements.

They try to be all things to all people.

You niche your business.

They deliver mediocre service.

You treat clients like royalty.

If you have time today, go do one of my favorite things:

"Shop" a health club.

See what they do. How they sell. What they offer.

After you see how impersonal they are and how they treat their members – go do the opposite.

You'll be on your way to building a great business.

Three Things You Need To Have A Successful Personal Training Business

To build a successful business, you need:

A Training System – If you don't have a training system you're not going to be able to build and maintain a successful business. Ever wonder why no one else talks about that? I do. If you don't have a training system for your business, it is kind of like marketing the heck out of a restaurant... without caring if the food sucks.

An Operational Systems – No operational systems mean that you'd better plan on running your camp or facility until you're 80.

No vacations, no sick days – no expansion.

If you want to ever grow beyond trading time for dollars – operational systems are a must.

Marketing & Sales Systems – This is the one that gets the most attention from everyone else, but without the other two – it can't create a successful business.

But if you have the foundation of the other two in place – the right marketing and sales systems are what propel you to a 6 or 7 figure business.

Honestly, most people don't do things that way.

Lots of sizzle – not much steak.

But the truth is that most 'business experts' in our industry focus entirely on #3 and ignore #1 and #2.

But I promise you… if you slight training and operations you'll be looking for the next fad or new get rich scheme before long while the trainers that mastered the trifecta will be thriving.

Are You Doing These?

Over the years - from my days growing up playing sports to my time as a college coach to my current professional life as an entrepreneur - I've seen 5 things that made people better:

Basic Studying.

I am a reader and always have been. My mom reads a couple books a week and it was instilled in me early. Maybe you prefer audiobooks, watching video, multimedia products…it's up to you. Most of the people I know that have become really good at something have this as part of their developmental arsenal. This is foundational in my opinion as it's something you can do literally every day if you choose.

Attending Live Events.

From camps as a kid to seminars and workshops now…these are incredibly valuable because they're immersive. You're not trying to fit them in between other work. I'm on my way to a small workshop today and I expect to get more from a couple days there than I would from studying the same material in a product format because I'll be free from distractions. I've often talked about the impact a couple of events early on in my career had on any success I've had - I feel sure that it can do the same for you.

Being Part Of A Group With High Performing Peers.

I've been part of some great Mastermind Groups and I've run what I'd argue have been some of the most successful groups in our industry. But I saw the power of this long before I was a professional.

All of the kids I played sports in the neighborhood with growing up went on to play a sport in college. Training and practicing with my best friend who was (still is) a tremendous athlete and had an unbelievable work ethic brought out the best in me. When I was coaching we had a really good team offensively and when new players came into our program they often thrived as offensive players - far exceeding anything they'd done in the past.

Maybe you can't invest enough (yet) to be part of a Mastermind Group like my Fitness Entrepreneur's Group…that's ok. You can still be part of a group of high-powered peers somewhere like Virtual Fitness Mastermind. You can connect with people there and set up your own meetings regionally.

Practice.

There are plenty of people who talk a good game on the internet. You need to be testing…practicing. If you want to be great at anything you need to practice. My guess is that the people you respect most in the field are the ones who are continually honing their craft. If you have a sports background you know the value of quality practice. My belief as a coach was that if I did a great job in practice, the games should be much, much easier.

Doing Work.

At the end of the day you have to put what you know into action. No theory. No armchair quarterbacking. That's why you don't see me writing about training based topics…I don't do enough of that these days to deserve your attention on the topic.

If you want to be good at something you have to put your skills and knowledge to the test. If you want to be a Transformation expert - then you need to prove that you can transform people. And if you're approach doesn't work when it's put to the test - then you adapt and improve. If you say you're a speed expert then your scoreboard is whether your athletes get faster. You improve with experience if you're willing to learn from it.

So take inventory of these 5. Are you making them all a part of your professional development? If not, what's missing? Improve it and you'll see a surge in your progress for sure.

3

Business Growth

Fitness Industry Problems: An Opportunity For You

No matter what industry you're in, problems create opportunities.

Walt Disney developed Disneyland in response to the fact that amusement parks left a lot to be desired.

Wal-Mart grew like crazy because retailers ignored markets outside the big cities.

If most of the fitness industry is going to ignore the problems at hand, then that equates to opportunities for you. Here are the most obvious opportunities as I see them:

Become "The Solution" For a Targeted Group of People In Your Area – Baseball players seek out Cressey Performance. People wanting to transform their bodies in Chanhassen flock to Justin Yule's Transformation Club. They each have their own 'who' and work diligently to attract them.

Determine who you want to serve and become the "go to solution" for that group. I know these people all built businesses by becoming passionate about helping a certain group and putting in the time to become the best solution for that audience.

If you take this approach as a businessperson, everything becomes easier. You know what you have to focus on, what to study, who to market to, and what your identity is.

I really think that the fitness industry is poised to move this way – targeted solutions for specific audiences. It's up to you whether you'll be one of the leaders.

Build a Community – All the gyms I just mentioned have their own community. Starbucks coined the idea of becoming their customers' 3rd place – that place people wanted to be outside of home and work.

Great fitness businesses become that 3rd place for their clients.

I mentioned it before. I don't care if you love or hate CrossFit, but they've built a community. Their members are posting pics and videos all over their Facebook pages, communicating with other "CrossFitters" outside the gym and making their experience viral. Think that stuff happens at LA Fitness?

Find ways to connect your clients with one another. Encourage them to support each other. Instead of each client only being "your client" – they also become part of "your team" or "your family."

Do that and you'll be amazed at the impact on your business, and you'll separate yourself from all the other trainers and gyms in your area.

Be The Anti-Health Club – Even if you are a health club. Make everything personal. Know your clients... not just their names. Know about their work, their families, and their hobbies. Even if you run group classes, at least spend some one-on-one time with clients in the beginning to build relationships and learn about them. Then make it a priority to have periodic one-on-one contact with them regularly.

If other clubs want to try to be Wal Mart, then you can be the boutique location that everyone raves about.

Deliver Results or Find a Different Career – If you aren't focused on making the people you work with better, move on. You aren't doing yourself or anybody else any favors if you don't deliver results.

I've spent *a lot* of time in health club settings, and most trainers there don't work to improve at their craft, don't do assessments, don't design programs, and don't really care about their clients.

They just sell training and give workouts.

Take the complete opposite approach.

Study like crazy. Become a great trainer or coach, and accept that it will require a BIG investment (time and money) on your part to get there.

Do assessments, design programs, and care about your clients' success. Focus on delivering results.

If you happen to work in a big gym, then do this, and you'll quickly set yourself apart from 99% of the other trainers there.

Run A Business That's Tough To Beat – If you're going to be part of the solution in the fitness industry as an entrepreneur, that means you are going to have to run a sound business that's poised to compete successfully with the big box health clubs. Here are the components I think give you the best chance for success:

- A facility with a low overhead, having primarily an open floor plan without expensive cardio machines or selectorized equipment.
- A model primarily based around group training.
- A specific target market (or two) that you're trying to serve.
- The utilization of EFT billing.
- A dedication to having a community atmosphere.
- A focus on client results instead of client volume.
- Several different revenue streams.

All the businesses that I mentioned previously utilize most, if not all, of these components. They give you the best chance for success.

So there you have it – my formula for taking advantage of the problems the fitness industry currently faces. What do you think? Are you one of the leaders ready to step up and take advantage of the opportunities I've mentioned?

Want to Do What I Do?

This week I'll be spending a great deal of time on two separate projects.

The first is doing calls with almost 20 fitness entrepreneurs who have shown an interest in my Private Coaching and Mastermind Programs.

The second is filming the final parts of my soon to release Rapid Product Creation 6 Week Course.

My business isn't that different from yours…or at least the business that many of you want. I spend part of my time with in-person coaching and part of it working online.

In fact, to be more specific, it's probably…45% Coaching / Mastermind, 45% Products / Courses. The other 10% is strategy / advising / consulting for companies.

In truth, if I look at a lot of the fitness pros I admire the most - that's a blend they have too. Boyle, Durkin, Cressey, Robertson...the list goes on and on of people who blend coaching with online.

So if that type of hybrid model appeals to you, here's my (abbreviated) advice:

Step 1: Be Really Good At Coaching - I think this should be obvious, but it's not. There are a lot of people selling fitness, sports performance and business information online that haven't ever really coached. The may have sold stuff...but they've never built their livelihood on making someone else better.

Do that first.

Step 2: Figure Out Who You Want To Help - Don't be a generalist...be a specialist. You can always expand, but online you need to target a smaller crowd than 'everyone.' Whether you realize it or not - you have a niche locally...it's 'people who live within 5-7 miles.' So you need one globally too.

I've helped enough varied entrepreneurs to know that what I do would help people outside of fitness & sports performance...but by being a specialist for those crowds it was much, much easier to build my business.

Step 3: Find Out What They Want & Provide It - It's not about what you want to offer or what you think they need. You have to meet them where they are physically, mentally and emotionally and be the bridge to where they want to go.

Here's where I approach that differently than most...

I start coaching those entrepreneurs who opt in for this email from day 1. From the first email, my goal is to coach them...whether they ever invest even $1 with me.

I feel that if I do a good job, they'll trust me enough that when they want to get more involved coaching - they'll come to me.

Most people - regardless of field - do the opposite. They hold back.

They say 'join this and you'll get what you need.' Then once you enroll in that program they say 'this one is ok...but the really good stuff is actually in this next level' and so on.

I prefer to instead over deliver at each level so that someone feels like 'if I'm paying $29.95 and get all of this...I can't wait to see what I get for a couple hundred dollars.'

Step 4: Create Relationship & Provide Simple Solutions - This is my business philosophy in a nutshell.

Create relationships first. I've talked about the concept of making 'deposits' into people's 'relationship bank account'. Do that as well as you possibly can.

Then provide them with simple solutions that solve their problems and give them what they want.

I do my best to do both - but don't think you need to do it the same way I do. You need to play to your strengths to accomplish these same two goals.

I use writing and calls and face to face meetings to build relationships.

You do what fits you.

I'm trying to provide simple solutions for entrepreneurs to allow them to build their Ideal Businesses...offline, online or both. Again, you decide what you're offering.

Step 5: Stop Dreaming & Start Doing - You can't have a different outcome until you start doing things differently. If you want an online component to your business..,create it. Now. If you want to offer something new within your business - do it.

Using the online stuff as an example...I'd estimate that of the fitness entrepreneurs I've talked with who said they wanted to offer something online and develop that hybrid model...roughly 1 in 20 ever did.

What is really disappointing about that is that in so many cases, what they said they wanted to do and how they described what it would look like was better than the competing offerings on the market.

But those competing offerings were actually done and being sold...not just ideas.

So if having a hybrid model appeals to you - there is how you do it.

All the same stuff applies as with your offline business...you can't just have a good solution, you have to go get people interested and sell it...but this is my approach for doing just that.

Make These Commitments

If you want to grow you have to commit.

Anything worth having requires commitment...we tell our clients that same fact.

But commit to what...growing? Improving?

Yes - but let's get more specific for a minute.

I've listed out 9 different commitments that are more specific...commitments that, if you're willing to make them, will move you on the path to building your Ideal Business.

So...now the ball is in your court. Will you view these 9 as ideas or statements that you're willing to commit to?

- Each day I will communicate our value to at least one client or prospect who can buy from me — in person, on the phone, or least preferably, via a personal email.

- I will grow my business' list of clients and prospects, because if my list isn't growing, my revenue likely isn't either.

- I will commit to regularly e-mail value to my growing list. My communications will primarily focus on improving the lives of my readers, not selling, pitching or promoting.

- I will share the positive things my clients say about my business with others. I understand that if I say it, I'm selling. But if my clients say it, it's the unquestionable truth.

- I will understand that how I think is exactly how I sell and market. Because it's impossible to out-market or out-sell my mindset, I will focus on how I improve my clients lives rather than what I am selling them.

- I will approach business growth as the proactive pursuit that it is, and I will make time for it daily, even if only a few minutes - which is enough for real growth.

- I will be bold, because business is no place for the meek or modest.

- I will identify the approaches to business growth that I enjoy, and that generates results, and I will execute these because I know that if I don't like it, I won't do it.

- I will get clear about what my Ideal Business is and I'll pursue it daily.

These are commitments I make to grow my business that have worked for me and they'll work for you too if you're willing to make them.

The Magic of Value Capture [Your Secret Weapon]

Each time I hold my coaching meetings in Orlando, I take the groups to Disney Springs and they got to see first-hand what value capture is all about.

See, in the early 1980's Disney was capturing about 25% of what vacationers invested when they came to visit a park to now capturing over 75%.

It's the magic of Value Capture.

When someone sets out to vacation at Disney World they invest a certain amount to make the vacation not only happen, but to enjoy it as much as possible.

They spend on...

- Travel to Orlando
- Travel from the airport to the hotel or parking if they drive
- Food & Refreshments
- A Hotel or Resort
- Park Tickets
- Additional Experiences - shows, tours, etc.
- Souvenirs & Shopping

At one point, Disney really only did a good job capturing ticket and parking revenue and were pretty average (at best) at everything else.

But a while back they got a new CEO, smartened up and started providing as complete a vacation experience as possible so that they could capture as much of the investment people were making to come to visit Disney as possible.

So how does this apply to you?

Well, your clients come to you to achieve a desired result.

Let's say it's fat loss.

Well, just like Disney initially only did a good job of capturing the investment from tickets and parking, most fitness professionals only do a good job of capturing the value from the 'workout part' of the fat loss equation.

But aren't the clients doing more to lose weight?

Nutrition obviously plays a key role. That's a must.

What about supplements?

Do they need tools like foam rollers or lacrosse balls to aid in recovery?

Would more accountability expedite their progress?

If you start thinking about their actual goal and what goes into it, you're likely only capturing less than half of the investment they're making.

Now will you ever capture it all? Nope.

Unless you plan to start selling them all the food they eat (I've been in that business too...but that's a story for another day), then you probably want to stick to the education, coaching and accountability they need for the time they're not working out and maybe some of the retail (supplements / foam rollers / bands / etc.) purchases they'll make too.

And if you do that you're up to capturing just about everything you can that 'fits' your business.

(For a point of comparison - Disney captures pretty much everything but flights...no Disney Airline...yet.)

So how do you do this?

Well, my buddy and Mastermind Member Rick Streb shares how you can capture as much value as possible when it comes to nutrition in his Nutrition Profit System.

In fact, he's got 5 different Systems you can use - so you don't have to fit into some one-size-fits-all box (my whole Ideal Business thing is rubbing off on him) - you pick what fits you.

A true win-win.

3 Immediate Ways to Grow Your Business

We all want to grow. We want to improve.

It's not complicated…it's just how we, as entrepreneurs, are wired.

So with that in mind, embrace the 3 tips below and make sure they play a big part in what you do on a daily basis…and you'll be well on your way to consistent growth.

1. Be Somewhere – To quote marketing guru Dan Kennedy, "You Can't Do Business Sitting on Your Ass."

You need to be out in front of people where opportunities can happen.

Be visible by getting yourself and your message in front of your ideal prospects.

So go connect in person. Get your message in front of the right people on Facebook. Be seen. Constantly.

You can't just sit in your gym, do nothing to get in front of new business and expect to grow.

2. Do Something – Everyone has ideas. Everyone has talents. Few act on them.

Many of the successful fitness entrepreneurs I know are there primarily because they took action, not because they were more talented or had a better idea.

They just made something happen.

In fact, more often than not a bad decision is better than no decision because it leads to action. It is easier to correct the course once you've actually started than it is to get started in the first place.

A good rule of thumb is to do at least one thing a day to bring in new business, even if you don't need any new business.

3. Be Somebody - You need to position yourself as the best solution for someone…not just another gym or trainer.

You need to stand out.

How?

Specialize. Get in the media. Write a book. Be different and be better.

And I've got a Bonus one for you…

Ask – If you want something, you have to ask.

If you want more clients, you have to ask for the sale.

If you want more leads, you have to ask for referrals.

When you meet someone that can help your business – ask for something.

Successful people like to be asked for their ideas, opinions, advice, help, and influence.

There are four simple things you need to be doing every day: being somewhere, doing something, be somebody and asking.

Do those and you're almost assured of business growth.

The Formula [Case Study]

I want to share a simple formula for growing your business...here it is:

1. Get clear about who your Perfect Client is.

2. Focus your marketing efforts on prospects who match that Perfect Client profile and ignore pretty much everyone else.

3. Nurture your relationship with those prospects, discover what they want and display how you can help.

4. Once they know, like and trust you, get them on board as clients and provide solutions to their problems and help them get what they want.

5. Repeat that formula over and over.

So let me show you how that works in the real world.

My Perfect Client is a fitness entrepreneur.

Not a general entrepreneur. Not simply a personal trainer.

A fitness entrepreneur.

So, I've focused pretty much all of my marketing efforts on attracting those people or people who are aspiring fitness entrepreneurs.

And once someone is on my list, everything I write is written specifically for them.

I try to deliver what they (you) want and also do my best to help.

So when I do offer something for sale like the 'Best Sales Month Ever' offer - it sold out in just a couple hours in spite of being a pretty significant investment.

Now if any of the elements of the formula leading up to making that offer were missing or weak...there is no way I'd have sold it out period...let alone in a couple hours.

So put the formula into action.

In fact, I spoke to a couple of fitness pros yesterday that I know will benefit from this greatly when they put it into practice.

The first thing they (and most of us) need to do is to dial in their 'perfect client.'

Think about this from the client perspective instead of the business owner perspective.

You're reading this now. Would you be if I wasn't writing it specifically for you?

Would you read it if I was talking about restaurants, dry cleaners, chiropractors, car dealerships and realtors as much as I was talking about fitness business owners?

I doubt it.

But once most of us put the 'business owner' hat on, we're afraid to narrow it down and say that 'I work with people 50 and over who want to turn back the clock, look and feel great' or 'I help busy moms get the bodies they want in the time they have.'

No, we settle for saying 'I'm a personal trainer who works with athletes, fat loss clients, people in pain, seniors, brides to be, busy professionals, toddlers, people who wear sweaters and anyone else with a pulse and a credit card.'

Not very appealing.

So really spend some time on step one in that formula. Cool?

Once you do that, it's like the first domino...everything else will fall into place when you get that right.

So who is your perfect client?

Client Getting Made Simple

If you want to accomplish anything, basically it boils down to this simple formula:

1. Set a target
2. Break down reaching that target into a few simple steps

Let's use getting more clients as an example.

Target: Get 10 New Clients In August

Step 1: Ask every current client for the names and contact information of 3 prospects in exchange for a branded T-shirt.

Step 2: Contact each of those prospects and offer them a free sample of what you do.

Step 3: Contact all former clients and offer them an incentive to start back with you.

Step 4: Attend at least 4 networking events in August, and add at least 3 people to your network at each.

Step 5: Offer those 12 people a free sample of what you do.

With that simple approach you should be able to get a minimum of 20 prospects in for a free trial or a couple free sessions. Of those you should have no problem converting at least half, and you will have your 10.

Now maybe you prefer public speaking or Facebook ads. Maybe you prefer the *Business of the Month* program. That's OK – the formula is the same. The key is being specific.

Set a specific target, and create simple but specific steps.

In the example, I specified how many clients I wanted to get (10).

I specified how many clients I'd ask for referrals (all of them).

I specified how many leads I'd ask for from each client (3).

I specified how many former clients I'd contact (all of them).

Finally, I specified how many networking events I'd go to (4) and how many leads I'd get from each one (3).

This approach not only gives me a goal for each step, but also it allows me to measure, which, in turn, allows me to improve moving forward.

If I determine that many of my clients wouldn't give me 3 leads, for example, that would mean that I needed a stronger incentive.

If I figure out that very few of my former clients are willing to come back in, I need a better offer.

If I learn that I'm only getting 2 new contacts at each networking event, I need to attend more events.

If I close fewer than half the trials, I need to tighten up my sales presentation, or I need to make the trial a better experience for the prospect.

If you're not being specific, you'll never figure out any of this. You'll be stuck just guessing what you need to do next.

So set a target and some simple but specific steps to get there, and you'll suddenly see the business side of what you do get easier and your number of clients grow month after month.

14 Surefire Ways To Grow Your Fitness Business

1. Be Great At What You Do– If you're a terrible trainer or coach, all the marketing advice in the world won't make up for it. Think about seeing a great ad for a restaurant. It might get you in the door for one meal, but if your meal was bad, would any amount of advertising ever get you back?

2. Joint Ventures– Have you ever taken the time to find out how many businesses there are in your area who serve your potential clientele? You should. Build a relationship with them so you can eventually have them as a referral source. Start by being nice, offering free training to the owners and at least steep discounts to the staff. Send them some referrals. Eventually you will be able to get referrals and even more structured lead generation activities in return like endorsed mailings or emails.

3. Public Speaking– Incredible business builder. Why sell to one person when you can sell to 20, 30, 50, 100, or more at one time while also being positioned as an expert. There is no shortage of groups, clubs, and organizations looking for speakers, so don't ignore what is probably the best lead generation opportunity available to you.

4. Reactivating Old Clients and Old Prospects– These people already know you and have shown an interest in what you offer. Some of them have even worked with you. Go back to them with a special offer, and grow your business.

5. Networking– There is nothing better than face to face marketing. There is no postcard, e-mail, or newspaper ad that can compare to talking to someone in person. *Make a point of meeting several new people each day and adding them to your personal network.* Get out from behind the computer, attend networking events, and put yourself in more settings with people outside of your inner circle.

6. Up Sells and Backend Sales– There is NO ONE better to sell to than your current clients. If someone is purchasing a training program from you, *make them an offer at the point of sale* and upgrade them to a nutritional coaching program, a supplement package, or an accelerated training program that will compliment what they've already purchased. Don't hesitate to create new stuff to sell to the same people that have been buying from you for a while. You'd be amazed at some clients' appetites for new offers.

7. Hustle– Nothing gets done without hustle. We regularly host live business coaching events such as Bootcamp Bootcamp, and many of our star students regularly attend. They come from different parts of the country (even other parts of the world), and some have facilities while others don't. Each of them have honed in on 2-3 core strategies that have built their businesses – and it's a different 2-3 for many of them.

But the one thing that is the same for all of them is that they hustle!

8. Social Proof– You can never have too many testimonials. It is a great way to recognize clients' successes, and you never know which one will resonate with the prospect you're talking to, so have a lot.

9. Referrals– You should make referral generation your key marketing strategy. It only takes 4 things to make this happen. 1) A great service that people want to share. 2) You asking for referrals from EVERYONE– no exceptions. 3) You making it super-easy to refer prospects to you. 4) You rewarding people for directing prospects to you.

That's it, and as you noticed, the burden falls squarely on you, not your clients.

10. Risk Reversal– There should be zero risk for someone to do business with you. Free trials, 100% or more money back guarantees, short term entryway programs like a 21 Day Drop a Dress Size programs – they're all great ways to eliminate the risk for the prospect.

11. Invest In Yourself – Go to events like Perform Better Summits. Invest in educational products and programs, and get a business coach or mentor.

In fact, I don't know any successful fitness pros who haven't gotten some form of coaching or who haven't belonged to a mastermind group. That's not an accident.

12. EFT Billing- You didn't get into this business to be a bill collector, did you?

13. Sell Memberships, Not Sessions– Too many trainers sell a series, blocks, or packages– all a bunch of short term offerings that make it tougher to have a sustainable business with steady cash flow. Don't be one of them.

Sell your programs as monthly memberships where clients invest a set amount each month for a defined amount of service. Ideally this membership will be for a commitment of several (or more) months or will at least auto-renew every month.

14. Care About Your People– Your clients. Your network. Your staff. Make it readily apparent that you care about them and their success every chance you get.

Making Your Fitness Business Viral In Four Steps

Step One: Your Marketing Message – Your "message" is what you communicate to your existing and future clients, and this can sometimes have an impact on what your clients say about you. The areas to improve in your message are your *brand*, your *sales and marketing materials*, and your *values*.

Your Brand

Your brand is your company identity in the eyes of your clients. Branding is a big topic, so for now, it's important to know that you can and should improve your brand. However, once you have a good brand message, you should stick to it. If you change all the time, the "branding effect" will be greatly reduced.

Further, make sure that all your marketing materials include your brand – as it will become your business identity and will be what is conveyed when people spread the word about you.

So what is your brand?

Your Sales and Marketing Materials

Your sales and marketing materials include any form of communication that your clients or potential clients may see. You're thinking business cards and websites, but this also includes sales scripts, T-shirts, lead boxes, and anything else that spreads the word about you.

While getting "viral" is bigger than your sales materials, at some point your potential client, even if driven by word of mouth, will come in contact with these materials. The more "right" you get these materials the better, of course.

Continually improve the effectiveness of these messages by focusing on the changes that are the easiest and/or have the most impact.

Your Values

Your "values" are what you stand for as a business. I mean, what you *really* stand for. There are a great many fitness businesses that profess that they stand for a great number of noble things, but their actions prove otherwise. Whatever your values are, they will most definitely be communicated to your clients either intentionally or unintentionally. In fact, the unintentional communication, that is, the kind of communication that occurs by just being who you are, is perhaps the most significant. So what are your values?

Step Two: Quality of Service – At its core, this is what your business is. You exchange your training for your clients' money. The greater the value you give to your clients in exchange for what they give you, the more likely they are to be delighted, and that delight translates into your business going viral. But that's only part of the picture.

Giving someone high value for their dollar is a great start, but may not be enough to get people to talk about you. To do that, you need to be so excellent that you are buzzworthy, or, to put it simply, worth talking about.

Go beyond what they ask for when they become a client.

Be something so amazingly great that people will slap themselves and say. "Wow!"

Have you ever done business with someone that was "so damn good" you had to tell someone about it?

You should continually strive to improve, but remember there are times you need to stop making big changes and focus on small tweaks that most people won't notice. At that point your services will have become such an integral part of your message that they should not be publicly changed.

Constantly improve your training knowledge and the quality of your programming, but remember that clients also want a consistent experience – especially if it works.

Step Three: Client Experience

Some businesses make themselves buzzworthy with just the power of the client experience they provide. Domino's Pizza, for example, did this by being the fastest pizza delivery in the world. Not great pizza – but that wasn't their brand.

If you are excellent in both your quality of service and client experience, you are well on your way to going viral.

Here are some ways you should be constantly improving your client experience:

1. Shorten Your Client's Path Between Their Problems and Solutions – Get them results faster than everyone else.
2. Make the Process of Doing Business with You as Easy as Possible – Use EFT, answer the phone quickly, reply to emails in a timely fashion, and treat people the way you'd want to be treated.
3. Treat Your Clients with Respect – Respect their time, their effort, and everything else about them. Remember that they trusted you in what is typically an insecure time for them.
4. Make it More Than a Workout – They can get workouts at Curves, Bally's, and any number of other places. You need to provide atmosphere, energy, motivation and a genuine sense of caring.

Step Four: Referrals

Referrals can be broken down into two categories:

- Incentivized
- Inspired

Inspired referrals are the viral payoff we're discussing here– the kind that comes from giving your client an extraordinary experience.

Incentivized referrals come from JV's, contests, rewards, etc. Inspired referrals will come by addressing the other 3 viral key areas of improvement. In fact, a great business that excels at those three areas alone can build a great client base founded on going viral.

Incentivized referrals, however, give your business a great boost too, especially as you're still positioning yourself as the expert in your community at a very low cost. But in general, you can't expect to build a business solely from incentivized referrals.

Unfortunately, most of the talk about referral marketing only focuses on incentivized referrals and the short-lived fireworks they can provide. Don't get caught up in the hype and think that those alone will carry you.

So remember, focus on your message, extraordinary service, and the client experience. Once you are in a process of gradually improving those things, then add in incentivized referral programs in any of the following ways:

1. Point of Sale Referrals

2. Contests

3. Rewards

4. Gift Certificates / Gift Cards

5. Bring-a-Friend

Just remember that when you "bribe" your clients (let's be honest, that's what you're doing here), you can create a rather unsavory dynamic between your clients and their friends. Take care with how you do this. Most people do this in a sort of "pitchy" way. That is to be avoided. Try to make these programs fun – and try not to make the client feel pressured.

So that's it – follow these 4 steps and start taking your business viral!

3 Ways to Grow Your Ideal Business

A long time ago I learned Jay Abraham's 3 ways to grow a business...

You can get more customers...

You can increase the transaction amount with each of those customers...

You can increase the number of transactions with each of those customers.

I'm sure you've seen me share some variation of that and you've probably seen others share some variation of it too. I wanted to help you think about it in a really practical way...so here's how I see it:

First is to get more of the clients that you truly want to work with. You have to get clear about who that person is...then you have to get them to experience what you have to offer. Take a look at clients you're currently working with who fit that profile...your Ideal Client.

Then learn about where they are when they're not with you.

Where do they live?
What do they do?

Who are they friends with?

Where do they work?

Where do they shop?

Where do they engage online?

Then find ways to get your message out through those channels so you can be in front of others like them.

Referrals

Facebook Ads

Strategic Alliances with businesses that they frequent

Lunch & learns with their businesses

Direct mail to their neighborhoods

Marketing materials wherever they are

Get them in to experience what you have to offer and why you're the best solution for them.

Second you need to get them to invest more with you. How do you do that? By being a specialist rather than a generalist. By being a complete solution instead of just selling workouts. By giving them the coaching, the accountability, the nutritional support, the motivation, the experience and the results they both want and need.

You can charge more for this as your fee for service since you are both better and different than the competition and you can offer a la carte solutions to provide as complete a solution as possible.

Third you get those clients to stay longer. The best part of the 'third leg' of growing your business is that if you did everything I shared during the first two, this will largely take care of itself. If you are giving the client the results they want and an experience they love...they'll not only stay but they'll also become an ambassador for your business.

So that's it...3 ways to grow your business. Go put this formula in place and your Ideal Business will be yours before you know it.

A Simple Way of Thinking About Things

A simple way of thinking about growing your business is this:

1. Connect
2. Deliver
3. Multiply

Every training business has to address these three phases to optimize their growth.

The Connect phase is finding the clients who are qualified, whose needs and wants or pain you can solve in the most efficient and effective way.

The Deliver Phase is where you are providing a service, adding and delivering value, and also marketing and planting seeds for future business.

The Multiply Phase is where you are nurturing that lifetime relationship with people. Most people miss this part and go back to the before unit without utilizing people that already know and like what they do.

If your intention is to Optimize these 3 phases, you have to start at the very foundation. From the start, you have to create a world-class experience for your Perfect Clients such that they will feel confident and comfortable enough to refer their friends.

Connect

Before someone becomes a Client, and actually enjoys the Experience, you have to know who they are and what the steps are to provide them with the Experience that will give them what they want…and more. It Starts With You.

You need to be a leader for your clients. People are looking for someone who knows their needs and can provide a solution of the easiest way to get there. Most of the time fitness business owners just give out their information like:

"I'm a personal trainer."
"My programs are 3 days per week."

"We do metabolic training with kettlebells, bands and bodyweight exercises."

"It's $149 per month."

That's like Starbucks saying…

"We're a coffee shop."
"We're open from 6am to 9pm."
"We serve coffee."
"We serve it in cups. It's made from beans and water and stuff."
"It's $4.95 per cup."

Pretty appealing, right? You connect with your Perfect Prospects by talking about the unique problems, needs and wants they have and how you're the best possible solution for them.

Deliver

The Deliver Phase really starts when you are in a consultation or Success Session with someone. At that point, it could go either way. You want to make sure you are not simply selling training to them…but instead providing the best solution to them.

Begin with the End in Mind. Ultimately, that's what they want…the perceived 'end'. Show it to them. Talk about it. Then simply explain how you'll work together to get there. Then finally…go do what you do best. Deliver it and do it in a way that makes it fun for them. Makes it 'special' for them. Make them feel like they're part of an exclusive group. If you are leading them toward their desired result, and doing so in a way that also is wrapped in a great experience, you are going to create a happy client.

Multiply

Once you've attracted your Perfect Prospect and transitioned them into being a Happy Client, you can get them to refer to you...or basically Multiply.

Just think of it in this simplified way...

In order for a Client to refer a friend, the following three things need to happen:

1. Notice Conversations - Anytime someone makes a referral, it was because it came up in a conversation about that topic. You refer your friend to the restaurant you enjoyed because they are heading to dinner tonight and are not sure where to go.

2. Think About You - Once they've recognized the conversation is about something you are the Perfect Solution to help with, that has to trigger a thought of you. The best way to do this is by ensuring that their experience in step two, the Delivery phase, is phenomenal.

3. 'Introduce' You - If they've thought of you, they now have to introduce you and your business to their friend and actually make the referral. To ensure that they follow through on this next step, you have to make what you do (provide a result to a specific, Perfect type of Client) easy to talk about. So dial in your message, convey it

frequently and make sure they can talk about you and your business in a way that allows them to Multiply it.

That's the foundation of growing your business. Plain and simple. We can talk about a bunch of other things that play a role...but this is the core in the same way that training smart and eating supportively are the foundation for getting results. Everything else is secondary.

Everything.

4

Sales and Marketing

The Key to Better Marketing

The more I learn about marketing and selling the more I see that we make it harder than it needs to be. Fitness professionals typically choose one of two routes:

Route One: They avoid any consistent marketing efforts. They only market when they're in dire need of clients or when something falls in their lap. This is about 70% of the industry.

Route Two: This group tries a bunch of stuff, but it's more of a shotgun approach. They'll do some referral stuff, a press release or ad here or there. A little networking, Facebook Ads and anything else they think will bring in leads. They go wide but don't have much depth. This is about 20% of the industry.

For that last 10% - they're in the sweet spot. They are focusing on who they want to get and all of their efforts are directed toward getting those clients. If you want to fall into that 10%, here's what you can do:

Step 1: Figure out who you want to train.

Identify the top 20% of clients in your business and focus on them:
- What do they have in common?
- Where do they live?
- Why do they like training with you?
- Why did they come to you in the first place?

Get crystal clear on this. Don't cop out and say 'they're all different.' They're not. If your top 20% is 16 people, most of them might:
- Be Women
- Have Initially come for fat loss
- Be hard workers that enjoy a challenge and have embraced getting stronger
- Be part of households with incomes of $100,000+
- Have kids

If at least 2/3 of your top 20% have a number of similar traits – focus on them.

Step 2: Learn everything you can about them.

You want to know things like:

- Why did they come to you in the beginning?
- What do they love most about your business?
- What do they think makes you different?
- How would they describe you?
- What would they change about your business?
- Where do they live?
- Where do they work?
- What are their outside interests?
- What have they done before working with you?
- Do they belong to groups? Engage in hobbies or do charity work?
- Are they on Facebook or LinkedIn?
- Do they read? What?
- Where do they shop?
- What's important to them?

Learn everything you can learn (within reason).

Step 3: Build your Marketing Message around Steps 1&2.

When you're marketing you should always feel like you're speaking to one person...because you are. You may be speaking to one person 10,000 times over, but for each of them the message has to be personal. So figure out who that person is and what will appeal to them to get them to come in your doors.

The most valuable 2 things this message should have:
- Plenty of benefits that are really important to them.
- Detailed social proof from people like them.

Web copy. Ads. The way you describe your business. All of it needs to be specific, not general.

Step 4: Get the Message In Front Of The Right People.

Once you know who those people are, this should be much, much easier. You know a lot about your target market from Step 2...so use that to go find more people like them. You can:
- Target media that your market watches or reads
- Target them on Facebook
- Create Joint Ventures with businesses that attract them.
- Do neighborhood marketing where they live.
- Speak or network with the groups they belong to.
- Develop referral promotions that get clients to bring them in.

Just as importantly – you can say no to all those things that aren't bringing in those people. This approach will give you focus.

Step 5: This is optional...but very effective: Become Magnetic.

Marketing can be 'push' or 'pull'. Push is more like door to door selling. It can work, but you have to knock on a lot of doors. Pull is like having people lining up to come to your door. If you want to become Magnetic (i.e. – Pull Based) then you need to become an Expert Specialist for your target market.
- You need to write a book that is a hook for that market.
- You need to speak to groups they belong to.
- You need to have a lot of social proof from people they relate to.
- You need to get on TV, in the paper and on the radio.
- Write for local magazines or popular blogs. Get media credits.
- Position yourself so people seek you out.

Once you do that, marketing is a breeze.

So there is the way that I think you should approach your marketing in less than 1000 words. Is it really that easy…not exactly, but close. There is work – and a decent amount of it. But it's focused work that will make your business a lot more fun to go to each day and make marketing and selling stuff you enjoy rather than tolerate.

Put the five steps to work and dial in your marketing and clientele.

The ONLY 2 Marketing Strategies I'd Use Year 'Round

In the Producer Challenge I run to help fitness entrepreneurs grow their business and create a culture of driving production, I share an approach that I'd use to grow my business. It's called the Interval Approach to Marketing.

You sprint for a bit…3-6 weeks or so.

Then you go at a more manageable pace for a while.

So what's that more manageable pace look like?

For me it would center around 2 things…

Relationship Marketing

Email List Building

For Relationship Marketing I'd be doing a few referral things...
A Charity workout one month and a Bring-A-Friend week the next.
Using the Ask-For-Advice approach to relationship marketing once
a week or so.

Rewarding referrals that clients sent my way.

Informally networking or connecting.

If one of those felt like it was getting stale, I'd replace it with
something else that allowed me to build relationships with new
people and introduce them to what I do.

For Email List Building I'd be doing a few things as well...

I'd come up with a couple cool opt in gifts...probably one more
video based and one that was a PDF download.

I'd run Facebook Ads to one or both.

I'd share them through social media.

I'd post them on my site.

I'd find ways to get my clients to share it with their friends.

If I did local advertising, it would be to drive people to those opt ins.

I'd find other businesses to JV with and ask them to share one of
those gifts with their customers.

I'd set a weekly goal or two for Relationship Marketing – like how many people I could add to my list of connections and how many people I could get to experience what I offer.

And I'd set a weekly goal for new opt ins.

For me these two would go on for 52 weeks a year. Some weeks would be more and others would be less.

But my business would always be moving forward.

And when I was in a sprint…now I'd have a bunch of new people to market to because of my efforts during those slower times.

So if you're not sure what you should be doing when you're not marketing a Challenge or if you are just looking for a base to build on when it comes to your marketing plan, I'd start here.

K-L-T

You've seen it.

Maybe you fall prey to it.

Training businesses go hot and cold with their marketing.

They're aggressive or at least active in January and September or whenever things get really slow.

Then, when they get busy, they stop marketing.

They stop emailing their subscribers and nurturing that relationship.

They'll have a million excuses as to why…but the bottom line is that they drop the ball.

What they fail to see is that this approach turns a warm prospect into a cold one, by the time you get back around to marketing to them again.

Here's why this is a TERRIBLE approach…and why you see me in your inbox pretty much daily.

We can't know when our prospects are going to be ready for what we have to offer.

Because of this, we need to get to them way before they make that decision.

To be building a relationship.

See - marketing isn't about hard selling someone. It's all about getting a prospect to know who you are, like you and trust you.

And that isn't going to happen overnight.

Here are some things to think about:

Know: We get to know people gradually, through either an extended contact or many smaller interactions. Relationship Marketing works the same way. In most cases, a prospect isn't going to appoint you, their trusted authority, overnight…so you have to go with the "be present all the time, so when they need/want you – you're there" approach.

That is the essence of Relationship Marketing.

Like: This is about being authentic. Will everyone like you?

Nope…but you don't need everyone.

You just need enough of the right someones.

Here's the tough part about this though. They have to not only like what you're offering but they also need to like who is offering it.

So be you.

Trust: Trust is the cornerstone of actually transitioning someone from prospect to client. How do you get them to trust you? It's simple…be honest, be consistent & dependable and give value.

Since you're reading this…you already know that I try to develop these 3 through the newsletter I send you.

In fact, I think that the newsletter is about as valuable a tool as you can use to develop K-L-T.

The Psychology of Selling

I often promote some of my offers by using a deadline where you have either an opportunity to buy before the price goes up or you can join a program before enrollment closes.

So why does that sort of thing work and how can you use it to your advantage?

Well...it works for a couple of reasons:

1. People are conditioned to respond to deadlines.

From waiting to do assignments until the last minute in middle school to cramming for tests in college...we've always been conditioned to respond to deadlines.

So if I say 'the price of VFM is going up eventually. No deadline. Fewer sales.

If I just say 'go join VFM'...some sales, but again, no surge.

Add the deadline and sales jump.

But there is a second piece to that...

2. Pain of Loss.

We are far more fearful of missing out on something that we are excited about gaining something.

So if the price goes up Friday people don't want to miss out on saving. They don't want to lose out on the opportunity...so more of them take action than would have otherwise.

Combine the deadline with the potential pain of losing and you have a strong incentive for people to buy.

So how should you use that?

My suggestion is that you have a couple points of entry into your business...an evergreen one that people enroll in at any time...and a deadline driven one.

So if you run Transformation Challenges 4 times per year...you now have 4 deadlines that will cause people to act.

They enroll by a certain date or they miss out.

You probably get that concept already...good.

But if you're like most fitness entrepreneurs, you don't push the deadline as much as you should.

You get caught up in getting people ready for the Challenge and your day to day that you miss out on promoting the deadline...and because of that you miss out on a lot of people enrolling.

When I run a 3-4 day promotion...50-60% of the sales come on the last day unless I added a 2nd deadline with a fast action offer on day one (see how I'm using 2 deadlines to drive sales sometimes).

But I almost always send 2 emails on 'deadline day' and most fitness entrepreneurs don't.

Why do I do it?

Because people are busy. They have stuff going on.

I need to keep it in front of them.

And so do you.

Are you worried about offending someone that isn't buying?

If so...understand that offending someone who is actually costing you money (if they're on your list they're an expense...it costs money to acquire and manage email subscribers) is a small price to pay to connect with the people who actually are ready to work with you.

So use deadlines.

Promote them aggressively.

People often need that sort of nudge to get off the fence.

Yeah, we all want to work with super-motivated people...I hear it all the time.

But guess what...if they were super-motivated all along they probably didn't need us all that much.

So if you can give them a little push and then show them some results...that motivation with grow.

And a deadline can be the first domino in the process.

Leveraging OPA

One of the biggest opportunities you have as a fitness professional is to leverage other people's audience. Other businesses have worked hard to build up a customer, client, or patient base, and with a strategic approach you can benefit from that relationship.

A Perfect Example

Outside of our industry, my good friend Nick Nanton has done this about as well as anyone could ever hope to do so. Nick and his partner Jack's business model is actually pretty simple: They develop unique, high-value offerings that would benefit – but aren't already being offered to – the audiences of the colleagues they have (like me as an example).

They've created offerings like group-authored books that they guarantee to turn into an Amazon Bestseller, TV shows that allow people to gain valuable media credits, and even promotions that showcase participants in places like USA Today and other major newspapers. They've even recently developed an offering in which they film a documentary for clients and get it aired on the Biography Channel.

Then, Nick comes to someone like me and tells me about the offering to see if it would be a good fit for the people I work with.

If it is, he and I work together to introduce it.

Nick reaches a new audience that he didn't have to take years to build, and we get to share something of value we wouldn't have been able to otherwise.

How You Can Form Valuable Partnerships

Your approach won't likely be exactly the same as Nick's, but you can certainly borrow from the general premise. Here are 2 simple strategies that will allow you to leverage other people's networks that can dramatically build your business:

1. Easy Strategic Alliances - I've always been a fan of strategic alliance relationships between businesses, but usually these get bogged down when they rely on partners having to do too much work promoting each other's businesses. When this happens, the partners don't see enough immediate return to keep putting time and effort into the relationship.

The Easy Strategic Alliance Method eliminates that problem completely. With this approach you need to simply have 4 things:

• A Willing Strategic Alliance Partner: You should be able to find these in your network: business owners who are clients, clients who are spouses of business owners, fellow Chamber of Commerce members, or simply people in your network that own or manage a business.
• A Downloadable Gift You Can Offer: A healthy-recipe guide, a collection of fitness tips, a series of exercise videos, or something else of real value that you can give away digitally to the

SA Partner's audience. If you don't have anything like this, you can create your own, purchase private label rights to one, or get someone to create one for you (like the book of recipes). In fact, if you own Instant Fitness Copy or are invested in ClickFunnels through me, you can just use one of the ones I've provide to you.

• A Simple Squeeze Page: You need a squeeze page where the SA Partner can send their audience to access the gift while opting into your email list. If you have any technical knowledge, this is a 20-minute task. If not, you can go to Fiverr.com, UpWork.com, or Guru.com to get it done for you inexpensively.

When someone opts in at this page, they should be subscribed to your email list.

If you don't currently have an email provider, ActiveCampaign.com would be my recommendation.

• An Email That the SA Partner Can Send: You want to make this as easy as possible for the SA Partner, so you provide a pre-written email that is written as if it's coming from them. They can edit it as they see fit, but this approach will make it 10 times more likely that they'll actually send it out and that it will get a good response.

Once you have all 4 of those components you simply tell the SA Partner that you'd like to send a free gift to their audience as your part of the relationship. The SA Partner doesn't have to do anything but paste the email into the service they use to send broadcasts and press send. They also get the benefit of being able to give something of high perceived value to their audience to further enhance their relationship while having to put out no work or money of their own.

Once the SA Partner sends out the email, their work is done (unless you send another offer at a different time). You've eliminated the middle man and can now communicate with their audience without them having to do any additional work – the area where SA relationships usually fall apart.

Obviously, you still need to reciprocate with the SA Partner to make it a win-win, so if they want to take the same approach with your list, great. If not, they can do one of the more traditional tactics like giving discounts, providing gift cards, or sharing marketing materials.

2. Advertising 2.0 Media outlets like radio stations and newspapers have fallen on hard times when it comes to selling advertising, yet most have still never embraced the value of the email list they have.

With this in mind you can approach them and tell them that instead of purchasing an ad on the air or in the paper, you'd rather send an email to their email list. Tell them you'll provide the email (that they can approve) and all they have to do is send it out.
Negotiate the price, as you can likely get an email sent (that will have far more value) for less than it would cost to purchase an ad.

Once you've found a media outlet that's willing, follow the same steps you took in the previous strategy. You'll pay for an email once, but you'll be able to market to their subscribers and listeners who opt in again and again.

Either of these strategies has the potential to provide you with a number of high quality leads and an influx of new clients – all by leveraging the relationships that businesses already have with the people they serve.

How to Dominate Your Market

The first person to market often does well.

Not always...but often.

Maybe they create a category. If the market is ready for it, then it will do fine.

If it's a little ahead of its time...well, it won't go over as well.

But the people who really thrive are the ones who redefine a category.

The ones who create a new, more inspiring vision of what being in that category means.

They redefine expectations, making themselves the visionary leaders in their market...and then everyone else is left trying to catch up to them.

So how can you do this?

How can you dominate your market?

By redefining what it means to work with a fitness professional for your perfect prospects.

By raising the bar.

Give more.

Be better.

Be unique.

I'm not trying to be vague…but the answer will vary as to how you redefine your category depending on what you want to be known for, who your perfect prospect is…and who you are.

But if you decide to think bigger than you've been thinking and if you decide to redefine what running a training business for the people who you want to work with looks like – then you open up a world of possibilities.

Here's a simple way to get started on your plan to dominate your market…

Step 1: Figure out what are the BIG results your perfect prospects want and the type of experience that they would enjoy.

Step 2: Look at everyone in your market serving these people you consider perfect prospects and determine what they're falling short in. What do they miss?

Step 3: See how you can address those areas in your business.

It's a simple plan…but a plan that will work if you do it.

Will you?

Here's an example of how I've tried to do just that:

Step 1: My perfect prospects are fitness entrepreneurs who want to stop settling and finally build their Ideal Business. The want to have someone help customize a plan for them and help them achieve their goals rather than being 'fit' into someone else's plan for what their business should be.

Step 2: Everyone else offering coaching programs, licenses or franchises either tries to make everyone else fit into their one-size-fits-all system or they simply sell tactics and leave the fitness entrepreneur to figure out how the tactics fit into their plan. The others in my market miss that this is about the individual fitness entrepreneurs and what their Ideal Business is.

Step 3: I start at the fitness entrepreneur and their goals and work from there…I don't begin with a single solution and try to fit people into it. Everything I offer begins with that in mind.

That's a short summary that hopefully gives you an example of how you can do this for your own business. I won't bore you with the specifics of how I go about redefining my category…but this at least gives you a start.

How to KILL Your Brand

A long time ago, email marketing was explained to me using the analogy of a bank account.

When you deliver great content, you're making a deposit.

When you try to sell, you're making a withdrawal.

I adapted this analogy to the relationship marketing that I talk about so often...mainly because I've found it to be almost 100% true.

Well, this week a presenter used the same analogy to talk about branding.

He said that branding is anything that makes a deposit in the relational bank account and selling is anything that makes a withdrawal.

You know why this way of presenting this concept is so powerful?

It's simple.

It's easy to understand.

We see people pound our inbox with sales messages.

Maybe it's a mix of hard sell and soft sell...or maybe it's entirely 'Sale, Sale, Sale...everything 25% off' with no soft sell mixed in.

Do you have a relationship with those businesses?

Sure - you may buy something if it's cheap enough or if it fills a big enough need...but do you know, like and trust them?

Compare that with the business that gives, gives, gives...and then makes an offer.

Does that business have your trust?

Are you more likely to buy - even if you're not sure that you have a huge need or if the price isn't drastically discounted?

If you're like most people, the answer is yes.

If you want to kill your Brand - one of the fastest ways to do it is to screw up the ratio of adding value and extracting value.

If you're selling via email...are you sending awesome content and connecting with people via email too?

You should be.

I feel that this is one of the most important things I do...but before you think I'm going to just sit back and pat myself on the back about it, hear me out.

See, I've long believed that I share enough content for free to allow someone to build a tremendously successful business - if they just apply it.

That's my 'adding value.' It's me 'making deposits.'

And it's probably why I've had a bit of success when it comes to getting fitness professionals to work with me in VFM, invest in courses and even join Masterminds.

But in my family's other business...Fit Yummy Mummy, this was a huge strength for a long time, but it actually became a weakness for a couple of years.

Holly used this same formula...give great content really frequently...then sell periodically...and it worked even better than it had worked for me in many ways.

Then, along the way as she was busy with other things and as I was helping her prioritize how to invest her 'work time' - almost all of it went into adding value for the members of her paid community...but not enough focus was given to adding value to the people who had yet to join that community.

So maybe 600 of 50,000 people were getting the type and number of relationship deposits that they should have.

Over time this showed...lower conversion rates when there was a promotion.

Fewer opens when a content email did go out.

All because the ratio of adding value and extracting value wasn't where it should have been.

Holly has done a great job in fixing that once we recognized it - and because if it her business is thriving...and I felt like a big dummy for not catching it sooner since that was my role in her business...but here's the scary part:

At its worst in that business, she was still delivering 10X the value that some of the marketers and business owners...many of them 'leaders'...are giving. If this were a bank account, many of the ones I see would have been over-drafted to the point the bank would have closed their account.

If you're falling into this trap of making too many withdrawals without making enough deposits...fix it.

Start giving some of your best stuff...and do it more than you think you should.

It may seem counter-intuitive, but here's what I've found to always be true in my own business:

If the free stuff is really, really good...they'll have no problem paying for the products, services and programs where they're a fit because they know that:

1. They can trust that you'll deliver and they already know and like your approach.
2. If the free stuff is good they (correctly) assume the paid stuff will be awesome.

That approach will build your relationships, build your brand and grow your business.

The 3 Funnels You Need

So I'm all about simplifying things.

By now you've probably figured that out.

So with all the talk about Challenges, Front End Offers and Funnels I wanted to distill things down to what you actually need.

You need (at most) the following 3 funnels:

Funnel #1 – Your Evergreen Funnel – this is your main offer that is going on 12 months a year. This is where typical prospects who are looking for the type of solution you offer can test drive what you have to offer.

Funnel #2 – Your Deadline Driven Funnel – this is the funnel you use when you run deadline driven offers like Transformation Contests or similar short-term offerings.

Funnel #3 – Your Lead Magnet Funnel – This is the funnel you're using to build your email list. All too often fitness professionals lose sight of the fact that if their list is growing with the right types of prospects – they're assured of their clientele and income growing too.

It's as simple as that.

You Should Be Selling This...

When I take people through the process of helping them build their brand we spend a lot of time talking about what they want to be known for and what they think their ideal prospects want.

See, most of the time they get so passionate about the process of what they do that they forget about the result the prospective client wants in the first place.

But the truth is that if you want to build a powerhouse business then you must sell people what they want...not simply what you do.

When someone goes to the doctor they do it to get well - not for the process of a medical diagnosis.

When someone goes to a restaurant they don't worry about the process that goes on in the kitchen...they want a meal and an experience.

You sell the outcome they want...and over time you can educate them on the process.

A perfect example of this is when you have a prospective client that is an athlete.

They're not as concerned with how much they can goblet squat or what they score on the FMS. You're the one who makes the connection between those and their goals.

They want to perform better on the field or on the court.

They want to get off the bench and be a starter.

They want to make the All-State team.

They want to get a scholarship...or in some cases a professional contract.

A pitcher wants to throw 90mph...

A golfer wants to hit it 300 yards...

A football player wants to run a blistering 40 time...

In fact, having spent the past 22 years coaching - I'd tell you that for most sports the most direct path to on the field or on the court improvement is to improve speed, quickness and agility.

All other things being equal, the faster athlete will be the one who gets the playing time, the awards and the scholarships.

In fact, a lack of speed pretty much is disqualifier #1 for opportunities to play in college or professionally.

Speed development is the athletic equivalent of fat loss...if you can deliver it, you'll be in demand because it's what most people want.

The OTHER Must Do Marketing Strategy

Relationship Marketing may not be as flashy as the stuff some people talk about, but it's as effect as ever - if not more. So I've shared some thoughts on Relationship Marketing below.

How To Employ Relationship Marketing

If you want to make Relationship Marketing a key piece of your business growth plan, you have to understand that it's about adding value...not extracting value.

Relationship Marketing isn't:
- Only talking to people when you're asking for a referral or a favor
- Going to a Chamber of Commerce Event or BNI meeting and talking about yourself constantly and passing out a stack of business cards.

It's basically building relationships. Adding value to others lives (they'll reciprocate). Making people aware of what you do and how you can serve them. So here are some tips:

Do The People Close To You Know What You Do?

I'm always amazed that fitness pros will ask me how to market but they've failed to educate those close to them on what they do. People generally lean on the people or businesses they're comfortable with and know rather than searching out and 'interviewing' a bunch of different solutions.

Do all of your friends, family members, neighbors and anyone else you have a relationship with know exactly how you can help them?

Make sure they do. Reach out. Start a conversation. Your career will come up. It doesn't need to be the primary topic. Facebook, personal emails, phone calls and visits for coffee are your friend. Blind copied mass emails are not.

Most people are passive about connecting with others, so you'll need to be the proactive one. Send real holiday and birthday cards and be sure to always send a nice note, or at least an email, for events like marriages, children, new jobs, etc. People really do remember these things.

You probably won't see much immediate gratification, but the business growth will come...I promise.

Have You Asked For Help?

My favorite way to get people to proactively spread the word or open doors for you is to ask for their advice. I know, when you think about how to market your business, asking for advice isn't the first thing that comes to your mind...but it works.

It's this simple...Tell them you're looking for new clients (or whatever you actually are looking for) and be specific. Tell them you'd really appreciate their advice. They'll help. They'll likely help more than you'd expect.

Are You Stepping Out Of Your Comfort Zone?

You never know where you're going to meet a new client or important connection. Increase your chances of doing so by being social when you're out in public. Talk to the person next to you in line at Starbucks. Start conversations. Ask questions. Listen.

Conversation is a skill, and most people who will never grow their business will ignore it and spend their time texting or tweeting instead of actually talking to the human beings around them.

Don't be like most people.

Sure - it's uncomfortable to talk to strangers. It's not easy. Neither is building a great business. If you're not willing to do one you're probably going to have trouble doing the other.

Are you going out?

Get out there and physically meet people. If someone wants to have lunch and you can spare the time, do it. If a friend is hosting an event, go support them. The best contacts are still made face-to-face.

Networking is unpredictable, and you never know who's going to turn out to be a great new contact.

Are you following up?

Meeting people is great. But to actually grow a business from networking you have to get people's contact information and follow up. Don't hand them a card and ask them to follow up with you. That's reactive. Success is exclusively the property of the proactive.

Follow up on it the next day with a short email or phone call.

How do you look online?

When you do meet new people, expect them to do their homework. Manage your online reputation. How does your website look? Have you finished your LinkedIn profile? Does your Facebook page represent you the way it should?

Here are some final tips for how to Relationship Market the right way:

- **Be Referable** - If you're great at what you do and people have a great experience working with you - they're more likely to help connect you.
- **Be Different (In a positive way)** - If you're like everyone else people won't talk about you. But don't mistake that for trying to stand out in superficial ways. Stand out by delivering an extraordinary experience or just being a great friend...not by acting like a fool.
- **Represent Yourself Well** - As a business owner you're always on stage. Remember that.
- **Give Sincere Compliments and Recognize People** - When you admire something about another person - tell them. When a client does something well - recognize them.
- **Listen & Show Interest** - Listen to what the people you meet are saying instead of just waiting for your turn to speak. Don't fidget, look at your phone and focus on the person or people you're talking with.

So, start working on your network right now. Ask for help, offer value, and maintain the relationships. And remember, the best build strong relationships before they ever need them.

Borrow My Success Secret

I think there are a few things that I do that have helped me achieve success...just a few. I think being a coach first and a marketer / sales guy second is one. I think making important concepts simple is one. I think focusing on individuals and their unique goals instead of one-size-fits-all stuff is one. And the other is connecting.

Really...it's 4 things. Not much else.

And with connecting...I prefer face to face...then phone...then email...in that order. But the vast majority of my connecting is via email due to the leverage of it. See, most fitness entrepreneurs want ways to automate their email...and I think it's a mistake. I think that your prospective clients and your current clients want to feel connected to you. They want to know you. To do business with you they're going to have to like and trust you too. For me...email has been the platform for that.

Blogging is cool, but every time you ask someone to take another step like you do when you say 'click here'...you lose a bunch of them. In fact, you lose most.

I've easily done 8 figures worth of business directly tied to email...and my approach isn't complicated, so I'll give you a quick overview here:

Step One: Show Up - If you want to get people to read, you have to put stuff out there. Consistently. I'd say that most people should mail 2-3 times per week. Yes, I do more but I don't have the luxury of seeing my clients in person a couple of times a week either. So have something valuable to share at least 2-3 times per week.

**Quick tip - If you don't like writing or aren't comfortable with it, but you want to make it part of what you do...just write. I really didn't like it when I started...not at all. Now I love to write.

Step Two: Make Deposits - I try to deliver value...even when I am selling. I truly believe that someone could simply create a file of all my emails, ready them like a success manual and have enough to build a really solid business.

I'll use the bank account analogy...when you give value you're making a deposit and when you sell you're making a withdrawal...your goal should always have your readers feel like there is a positive balance in the account...ideally a big one.

Step Three: Be Authentic - People want to know you. They want to connect with you. That's how trust is formed. The more I share the better the response. This is why just sending a boilerplate email is a bad idea. It might be good information but it doesn't create any connection with you or your brand. I talk about my family, my experiences...even some of the less enjoyable ones...because people want to know that I can relate to them...that I'm not some faceless corporation that is just trying to take their money. The same applies to you too.

Step Four: Simple Value - I love to offer up simple concepts and tactics that can be applied quickly...things that either change the way the reader feels instantly or impacts their business quickly. That means things need to be simple. For you...that could be something to motivate, educate or inspire...but it has to be usable and simple.

Step Five: Commit To Your Ideal Brand - I mail pretty much daily and share what I feel I want my business to be known for and address. I get emails each week with people saying I email too much or some unsubscribe...and that's ok. Those people might be awesome, but they're not my people. Commit to you and your brand...the right people will connect and the others will move on.

I often get asked...where do I get things to write about? The answer is everywhere. Conversations or meetings with clients. Personal experiences. Businesses I interact with and things I study. I really only write about a handful of things...the 20% that delivers the 80% of the results in building your Ideal Business...but I'm always looking for new ways to get my point across while staying true to my brand.

There's a quick overview on my approach to email marketing...hope it helps.

Creating Your Own Tribe

Right now I see so many fitness professionals who are great at what they do struggle to build a loyal community of clients who become true advocates for their business.

So, what I wanted to do was to give you a primer on how you can build your own Tribe.

Now, be forewarned, this will probably get into things that we don't often discuss – but it will be worth it.

So here we go…

First off – here is my definition of **Tribal Marketing**– The technique of using associations, clubs or groups to turn ordinary customers into loyal, raving fans **due to a shared set of beliefs and ideals.**

Think about this quote:

"People will do anything for those who encourage their dreams, justify their failures, allay their fears, never prove them wrong, confirm their suspicions and help them throw rocks at their enemies" ~Blair Warren

So how do you use this in business? You create an environment that…
- Allows people to belong to something bigger than themselves.
- Give them something to believe in.
- Creates an environment for their growth.

- Gives them social significance.
- Gives them peace of mind.
- Allows them to connect with a philosophy.
- Provides them with a feeling of prestige.
- Provides them with a unique experience.
- Gives them something to be 'special.'

There is plenty of overlap in those statements so you get the picture.

In short – you're trying to move people from basic members or clients to Members of your Tribe.

Customers care about products & services. Members of your Tribe are concerned with the human connection that comes with a certain product or service or philosophy.

So, I'm going to ask you to think about situations where you've considered yourself to be a member of something rather than just a customer…and member isn't the best word in our industry due to health clubs, but I'm going to use it since it's broad.

That and because people who see themselves as "Members" buy 66.3% more than people who just see themselves as customers.

So answer these questions:
- What Groups, Teams or Associations Have You Joined in Your Life?
- Why did you join?
- What's your most vivid memory of your membership?
- What did you or do you like most about that experience?
- Did you feel like you belonged to something unique? Special?

For me – some sports teams and coaching organizations have provided that. A couple mastermind groups have provided that. A feeling of belonging to an elite club where members were 'special.'

Some memories from these teams and groups have lasted for decades. You want to have that type of impact.

So how do you make this part of your business…here are the Key Components:

The Story - There has to be a backstory to why you exist. The more personal a connection you have with the ideal client or member – the better.

Your story should:
- Answer the question of why this business came to be.
- Give people a reason why they should identify with you and not your 'enemy.'
- Possibly create a bond between your business and your target market.

Your Philosophy & Mission – Hopefully this mirrors what your perfect client naturally believes in or it should at least strongly appeal to them. At the same time, it should repel people who don't fit.

This should be what guides your business, the standard against which all action is taken. It lets people know what to expect from you and embodies not only what you are today but what you aspire to be in the future.

Your Rituals, Habits and Culture – You should have your own rituals, things that people connect with. You should have your own culture. You need to establish your own types of common behaviors.

How do you cultivate it? It has to be done every day. You're creating a unified front and a set of behaviors that people not only adopt, but that become important to them.

Your Enemy – Every strong brand has a common enemy. Apple vs PC. Starbucks vs Dunkin Donuts. Republicans vs Democrats. Without Evil there can be no Good.

Your enemy could be anything that takes focus away from you or runs opposite to your philosophy…but you need to name them. Health clubs, trainers that think 'getting tired' and 'getting better' are the same thing. You pick.

Your Language - All great brands have this and using it well tells others you're one of them.

The Leader – People want to be led. This also makes second comers "me-too" copy cats.

How do you position yourself as the leader?
- You communicate through stories, personal and others. Success Stories.
- Invest heavily in your education.
- Walk the talk.

Blending all of these cultivates true fans. Putting all of these together creates believability, which causes people to want to belong.

If that seems overwhelming – just go item by item and try to decide what you want your business to be. Before long you'll have something that truly stands out.

And here are a few other tips:
- Quit trying to be like everyone else.
- What is your unique story – how can you blend it in? Why would it be important to your prospects and clients? Tell it.
- Create a language of your own
- Stand up for what you believe in and stand against what you don't. Middle of the road = weak.
- Celebrate the things you want to be part of the culture. People will catch on.
- Create some simple differentiators – CrossFit naming workouts was simple. At Starbucks, Venti is simple. Having a unique way to finish every session is simple. Add up a few simple differentiators and all of the sudden you're perceived as different as a whole.

I know this is a different way of thinking... but I have the feeling your wheels are turning. If not – re-read it. There are any number of businesses that have built loyal followings that generate word of mouth and referrals, are impervious to competition and have become part of their client's identity.

Why shouldn't your business be one of them?

Because if you get this right it will change everything.

Marketing Without Spending a Fortune

One of the most common questions I get goes something like this:

"How can I fill up my schedule without spending a fortune on ineffective advertising or direct mail?"

What they really mean is:

I don't have enough clients. Can you help?

Well, the better question is, "What didn't I do in the past few weeks to cause me not to have as many clients as I want?" I guess what I'm saying is the answer lies in *your own actions.* Every day you get to decide whether you're going to work on your business or just complain about the problems within your business.

So, with that in mind, here are several things you can do ASAP to get things rolling... if you're willing to take ACTION:

1. Evaluate your sales system

Without an effective sales system, an increase in leads isn't going to help you much. You need to have a systematic approach for presenting your offerings to your prospects that will give you the highest possible outcome when it comes to generating clients and increasing revenue. Here are some tips:

- Use a script. Every presentation should be the same. Develop your best approach, and use it every time.
- Use an alternate choice close. Present 2-3 options and ask the prospect which one they want to get started with.

- If your ideal offering is a 3 session per week bootcamp, make sure there is a 4 or 5 session per week option. This will make the 3 session per week option look less expensive by comparison.

Bottom line: bad sales system = bad income.

2. An easy way to ask for referrals

While you should have several referral systems in place, this one is probably the easiest. EVERY time someone says anything positive about your services reply with this:

"I'm so glad you're seeing great results and enjoy working with me. I enjoy working with people like you that are truly motivated to achieve their goals. (Pause) By the way, most of our new clients are referrals from current clients that are enjoying their experience with us – so if you're pleased with your progress please tell your friends, that would like to achieve similar results, about us."

Many will respond by saying that they've already told someone about you. If that is the case, then simply thank them for doing so by providing them with a gift card or certificate that they can provide to a referral.

3. An easy way to reactivate former clients

Here is a simple way to reactivate former clients. Go through your database, and call your former clients using this simple script:

"Hi _____, this is _____ from XYZ Personal Training. I just wanted to give you a call to see how you've been doing since your last session?"

If they say they're doing fine, simply say:

"I am so glad to hear that. If you need anything or want to come back in for a session, please give me a call."

If the response is something like, *"I've been slacking on my workouts,"* or, *"I need to get back on track,"* follow up with:

"Let's schedule you to come back in for a free session this week. Which is better for you, Tuesday or Wednesday?"

Remember, if people forget about you they can't refer.

4. Reaching out to local businesses

If you want to fill up your bootcamp with prospects fast, you can do a business call campaign. A business call campaign is probably not in everyone's comfort zone, but if you're willing to do it you are guaranteed to generate a bunch of new prospects in a hurry. The added benefit to something like this is that it makes your camp a lot more energetic with bigger numbers and really expands your network in a hurry. So here is what you do.

Pull out the phone book and turn to the yellow pages. Start with the 'A's' and begin calling all local businesses that might have an employee that fits your target market. Here is an easy script for you to use:

*"Hello, this is _____ from _____ and in celebration of our "Get (Your City) Fit Month" I wanted to call a few local businesses, and the **first person to answer the phone WINS A FREE TWO WEEK COMPLIMENTRAY MEMBERSHIP to my fitness bootcamp...***

AND THAT'S YOU!!!!!

CONGRATULATIONS!!!!!

*Now all you have to do is RSVP by going to my website and entering your claim number in the next 48 hours (have form or contact page) or by coming to camp orientation this Saturday at 10 a.m. to secure your spot in this month's camp... **Would you rather attend orientation*** *this **SATURDAY** or register through the website and attend the **orientation next week???** GREAT!!!! And your first and last name was? And I also need second phone number where you can be reached?*

*Ok _____, when you come to orientation, ask for **(name)** and it should take about 10 minutes to get you registered. And if for some reason you cannot make your appointment **(DATE/TIME)** – can we count on you to give us a call back at (number) with a better time?"*

If you commit to making a dozen calls a day, you'll get 3-4 people that want to take you up on your offer. Of those, 1-2 will show up to camp. Five days a week of that means 5-10 new leads a week, or 20-40 new leads per month.

Now, here's how you turn them into paying clients:

Following orientation or the first day of camp, show them that they can trade in the 2 weeks for one month free if they enroll in the next camp (or 2 camps…your choice) if they choose to during their first visit.

Even if you only convert 25%, that's 5-10 new campers per month. Not bad for a few phone calls.

So there you have it, four ways to add more prospects and more clients without spending a dime. And remember, these are in addition to the things you should be doing on a daily and weekly basis while executing your fitness business growth plan. If you're working a plan list, you should have no problem filling up your schedule in a hurry, with almost zero out of pocket cost.

7 Hidden Fitness Marketing Tactics

When discussing marketing it's easy to fall back to the standby stuff like networking, public speaking, direct mail and PPC ads.

But these are not the only ways to grow your business. Here are 7 hidden fitness marketing tactics that will help you grow your business in a hurry.

1. **Have a 'Carrot'** - One of the best hidden fitness marketing tactics I know is to build "carrots" into your business. Martial arts does this with the belt system. Most MLM companies have this with different tiers you can ascend through by reaching certain performance benchmarks. The easiest way to build a carrot into your business is to run transformation contests so your clients have a short term deadline to shoot for. But don't limit yourself to this. There are plenty of other ways that you can set intermediate goals for your clients so they can reach certain benchmarks to reinforce their successful behavior.

2. **Recognize** - Make sure you're recognizing your clients every chance you get... the loyalty it will build is enormous. Client of the week or month. Simple acknowledgment of a job well done. An occasional card congratulating someone on their accomplishments. All of these will help you build a fiercely loyal client base that will refer people to you over and over.

3. **Social proof** - People want to see people who've been where they want to go. Collect tons of testimonials, before and after pics, and success stories. Make them a key part of every website, blog, ad, and postcard and showcase them in your facility. This will close more people for you than the best sales script ever will.

4. **Continual improvement** - If you want to keep your clients excited, continually add new features, offerings and systems. This

will keep things fresh and keep your people from looking elsewhere for the "better mousetrap." Plus, these new additions are great for generating publicity and to use as marketing assets.

5. **Have a Hook** - People want to feel like the person they're working with is an expert in exactly what they need. If someone wants to become a better cyclist, they want someone who is an expert in coaching cyclists. If they're moms, they want a mom's fitness expert. Figure out your hook, and it will make everything else about marketing easier.

6. **Consistently soft selling** - You should always be building value in your other offerings. If you sell supplements – talk about the benefits, share success stories, and present it as a solution when the opportunity presents itself. You can do this without ever hard selling someone. You're just sharing solutions and successes.

7. **Over Delivering** - It goes without saying, but every day you have the opportunity to keep your clients excited about you and your business, so make sure that you do. You are delivering so much more than just results. You're delivering an experience.

Make sure the atmosphere is energetic and motivating. If you train in groups be sure to give everyone some personal attention. Send personal cards & emails. Make personal calls. Set yourself apart from every other business your clients interact with. You're guaranteed growth if you do.

So there are 7 hidden fitness marketing tactics that get overlooked more than they should.

3 Fitness Sales Keys to Remember

Selling personal training, group training, youth fitness programs, or even health club memberships...that is the foundation of your business. No sale means no client or member.

But most fitness pros I know hate selling, but that's only because they're not comfortable with it yet. Here are three tips to change that and make closing sales much, much easier.

Fitness Sales Key #1 – Everything Leads To A Sale

Sometimes I have to remind the fitness pros we work with that while sending press releases, getting on TV, making blog posts, writing articles, and creating products are great...they're all just a means to lead to you selling something.

See, sometimes we have to keep our eyes on the prize. Let's say you don't have enough clients. What are you going to do? Are you the type of person that will simply wait around for something to happen...or are you the person that will go out and make it happen?

When Holly and I were living in a basement, while we were getting our training business and health club ramped up, I was laser focused on selling training. I didn't leave the gym without getting two new clients. It meant some late nights, but like they say, when there's a will, there's a way.

Even before that, when I was first running a training department in a local gym, the company had a bonus of $250 if you sold 12 deals in a pay period. My goal every pay period was 36 deals, and I considered that $750 part of my regular income. I knew I needed 3 deals a day to make it happen and was relentless on getting those three. So, you can keep doing all those other things...blogging, sending press releases, writing articles, etc. But don't lose sight of the fact that selling is what pays the bills.

Fitness Sales Key #2 – Proper Framing Leads To Bigger Sales

Want an easy way to sell bigger deals? It's two simple steps, but I'm not sure you'll believe me if I tell you.

Step 1: Offer no more than 3 potential options to a prospect... something like this:

➢ 1 Session Per Week

➢ 2 Sessions Per Week

➢ 3 Sessions Per Week

It could be 2, 3 and 4, or it could be 3, 4 and 5. It makes no difference really. You know what you're currently selling. Just reduce it to 3 options.

Step 2: If your most popular program is 2 sessions per week but you want to sell more 3 sessions per week packages, add a package bigger than that to your price sheet.

If you already have:

➢ 1 Session Per Week

➢ 2 Sessions Per Week

➢ 3 Sessions Per Week

Then switch to offering:

➢ 2 Sessions Per Week

➢ 3 Sessions Per Week

➢ 4 Sessions Per Week

You'll immediately sell more 3 sessions per week programs. It's all simple psychology. Too many choices have been proven to cause indecision, and high priced offerings make offerings priced lower seem more reasonable. There you have it, two easy steps to more sales, bigger packages, and more programs sold.

Fitness Sales Key #3 – Sell Something

Get small commitments first. There was a time in my personal training career that I'd average three closed sales a day. Unfortunately, many trainers don't do 3 a month. The trick was to close the ones that weren't ready to commit to bigger programs on something smaller.

If I was doing a speaking engagement, I'd close the attendees on something small. Get a 'yes' first. Once someone has invested a little with you, it's much, much easier to get them to invest more...but only if you deliver great service during that initial purchase.

So, if you're having trouble getting people to enroll in "big ticket" programs, get them to at least invest in something small first.

Then, after you've built a little more rapport and have delivered great service and value, present your bigger offerings.

You'll be pleasantly surprised at how little resistance you get then.

This should help you get a little more confident and comfortable with sales.

The Right Way to Run a Business

Every year, Perform Better hosts some of the best educational events in the industry. Each time I attend one of these...I think about how much fitness professionals could learn from the Perform Better company.

I've attended over a dozen Perform Better events, so I decided to share some lessons I've taken away from doing business with them which could benefit all of our businesses:

- **Deliver Value To Grow Your Business**– I've attended about 10 Perform Better events, and every time I've felt like I've gotten more than my money's worth. In fact, to this point I've yet to come across someone who didn't feel like they've received their money's worth (or more) at any of the Perform Better events.

This kind of consistent value that they deliver is the foundation of their success and should be the foundation of any business's success. It's as simple as this: In every transaction you have with a customer or client, it is your job to provide them with an experience that makes them want to do business with you again.

- **Educate and the Sales Will Come**– The Perform Better Summits, their One Day events and now the workshops they host at their own facility are all incredible sales vehicles despite nobody ever really "pitching" anything. The key is simple. Each of these events educates fitness professionals on how they can do a better job serving their clients. This is a great way to generate sales in two ways:

  1. Any of the tools or resources used in the presentations are made available by Perform Better, so if fitness professionals want to implement what they've learned, Perform Better offers solutions so they can.

  2. The fitness industry is notorious for turnover so by educating fitness professionals, Perform Better is essentially helping

people stay in the industry, become more successful, and in turn, potentially become a long term customer.

How can you apply this? The more informed your clients are, the more successful they will be. If you educate them on nutrition, supplements, and a supportive lifestyle, they'll be more likely to reach their goals and will be more likely to stay with you as a client. Not only that, but since they will be more educated, they will seek out these other solutions like supplements or nutrition education, which you can provide for them as an additional profit center.

- **Make Everything A Win / Win**– This is similar to my first point, but I've dealt with Perform Better on a bit of a different level than most consumers, hosting pre-conference events, having them as a sponsor to my events and collaborating in other ways.

  What I've consistently seen from them is that in every transaction, every project, and in every working relationship, they work to make sure that both parties come out ahead.

  This sounds simple, but in business and especially in the fitness industry, it's not as common as it should be.

  They've worked diligently to make sure we benefit at every turn when we deal with them, and you should be doing the same in all your business relationships. You should make it a goal that every client, prospect, JV partner, or member of your network feels like when they deal with you, they benefit.

- **Keep Evolving**– Every year Perform Better Summits keep changing and improving. Each year there are new presentations highlighting the latest successful industry trends in training and equipment. In fact, the Summits are often the vehicle to educate fitness professionals on the latest industry developments, so they're usually the people setting the tone for a lot of what successful trainers and coaches are doing with their clients.

- **Use Relationships As Your Foundation–** We talk about it over and over, and Perform Better is a perfect example of it – relationships are crucial to business success.

  When I attend Perform Better events it feels kind of like a big family reunion – but more fun.

  This isn't an accident. Their team is incredible and takes a personal interest in everyone they do business with. In fact, it's pretty apparent in everything that they do from consistently looking for ways for you (or us) to save money when making purchases to little things like Chris Poirier – taking a couple minutes out from running the event – to have an iPhone Lightsaber battle with Tyler when he was young or a representative that we worked with having a baby gift for Holly when she was pregnant with Alex.

  All of this is stuff you can do as well. Take a personal interest in your clients. Be nice (and attentive) to their kids. Go out of your way to help them be more successful.

There you go – 5 big lessons you can take away from the equipment company I consider to be far and away the leader in serving the fitness professional market.

5

Referrals

3 Killer Referral Strategies

Physician Referrals: If you want to set yourself apart from other fitness pros in your community, send a health and fitness report to your clients' physicians. This professional courtesy is designed to create a line of communication between the doctor and yourself – and as a bonus, it positions you as a credible resource for the doctor when making recommendations to patients. The report might include the following:

- Weight
- Body fat Percentage
- Resting Heart Rate
- Blood Pressure
- Muscular Strength Assessment

- Flexibility/Mobility Assessment

Include whatever else goes into your assessment process. You can send this report each time you update your assessment. This single approach can set you apart from other fitness pros and fitness providers in the eyes of your community's medical professional.

Referral Stimulator Email: This is very simple to do. Just send a personal email to clients and ask for referrals. Here's an example:

Subj: *I Need Your Help!*

Dear Ms. Jones,

I think you can help me with a problem I have. I don't know if you realize it or not, but marketing for new clients can be pretty expensive. And after I spend all that money on marketing, I'm still not guaranteed to get one single new client.

"Word of Mouth" marketing is still the best type of marketing. And frankly, I'd rather reward you for sending me new clients than spend all my money on radio or newspaper. Many happy clients have mentioned that their friends, acquaintances, and family members have expressed an interest in improving their health and fitness. With this in mind, I came up with my new…

Referral Reward Program!

Here's how it works. For every referral that you send me who becomes a client, I'll give you 20% off of your monthly rate for the next 3 months.

So if you refer just 5 people you'll get your next 3 months of training FREE!

I know that I don't have to offer rewards for referring friends, but I think it's important to show that I value you as a client and appreciate your referrals.

When you think about people that you might refer, keep these ideas in MIND:

- *People you work with*
- *Friends listed in your phone or email address book*
- *Neighbors*
- *People you know from your hobbies and other interests*
- *Family members*
- *People you do business with*
- *People who attend your church*

Hopefully, that will jog your memory a little. If you just spend a few minutes thinking about it, I'm sure you'll come up with quite a few people you know who would like to experience all the benefits that you've experienced while working with me.

All you need to do is reply with the people you think would be interested in finding out more about my services and their contact information. I'll contact them and offer them a free gift of 2 weeks of my fitness bootcamp as a gift from you.

Thanks for your help and I look forward to rewarding you soon!

"Bring a Friend" Sessions: If you offer group training, this is the simplest referral system you can put in place. Just announce a "Bring A Friend Week" in which all of your clients can bring a guest free of charge to participate in a week of workouts.

Announce the event about a week prior to the actual day, and continue to promote it leading up to the event. You can combine this with another referral system and offer incentives or a preferred rate for any guest that becomes a client. Have a way to capture the contact information of each guest and continue to market to them via a newsletter or other promotional material. Have a free report and a special offer for upcoming events available to them at the conclusion of the session.

This works almost as well with standard one-on-one or semi-private training, it just takes a little more preparation for the actual sessions. You can develop a standardized entry-level program for the guests to follow for their workouts.

If you want to really take this to the next level, hold a contest with prizes for the client that brings the most friends during the week, and give them their next month free.

Now you have 3 easy to use referral strategies at your disposal. Pick 2 and plug them into your business next week so you can start getting these referrals rolling in.

12 Months Of Fitness Referrals

Every fitness professional knows the importance of generating referrals as it relates to business growth, so why do so many struggle to implement referral programs in their businesses?

My guess is that they don't set deadlines to implement what they know. So I'm going to set some deadlines for you. Here are 12 months' worth of referral generating ideas. All you have to do is follow the formula and watch your referral business grow!

Week 4 – Set up an ongoing referral program. If you don't already have one set up, you should do so immediately. There is no excuse now not to have an ongoing referral program in place. Simply come up with a reward that you will provide to clients and members of your network that send new business to you. The optimal approach is to reward the act of referring prospects to you and also reward the referring party when their referrals become clients.

Week 8 – Run a transformation challenge. Twelve weeks in length is a good starting point. This is a great referral generation machine because people will ask for help from friends and inevitably tell them what they are involved in. Don't hesitate to give away supplements as a prize.

Week 12 – Begin including a 21-day referral offer with all new client purchases. Include an offer that gives them a discount on dues for each new person they refer during their first 21 days.

Week 16 – Begin a campaign of integration marketing. While this won't boost referrals per se, it will get an influx of steady new prospects into your business. Integration marketing basically is trying to integrate your offerings into other businesses' marketing and sales processes.

Week 20 – Begin sending out birthday gifts to all your clients. You can collect their birthday at the enrollment process in an unobtrusive way, letting them know that you need it to send them a birthday gift. However, this should always be optional. On their birthdays, send them a gift card or some free supplements for themselves and a friend.

Week 24 – Set up a campaign associated with the next major holiday. Tell your clients that they and a friend will get a discount on a program or product during the holiday period.

Week 28 –Send out an email or card to all your clients saying that you're doing a new client drive this week and would like to know if they have any family or friends who would be interested in doing a free trial with you. Give them some kind of gift or incentive for every person they bring in. In addition, make sure that they have a gift card that they can give to their friends or family members to entice them to do business with you. In other words, you're not just having the client tell the friend about you, the client is giving a free gift card away that will bring them back to your business.

Week 31 – Add a bring a friend function to your business. If you run group training, this is easy. Just have a day or even a week each month where your clients can bring friends to their sessions.

Week 36 – Run another transformation challenge. Use what you learned from your initial challenge to make this an even bigger success.

Week 40 – Begin giving plastic gift cards to your clients. A plastic gift card with a magnetic strip on the back is a better tool than a coupon so it will set you apart from the competition. Your clients will then have the opportunity to provide these to their friends, and it will have a significant perceived value. Whenever a member of your network or a client provides someone with one of these cards this also gives them a chance to tell your story in a very unobtrusive and natural way.

Week 44 – Hold another referral contest. Incentivize your clients by giving them a cash reward or a big prize like a mini-vacation. Just think big and create a huge buzz. The possibilities are endless.

Week 48 – Conduct a one-time-only tell-a-friend offer or incentive. For example: Tell two to three friends about us, and you can get this free weight management class. The important thing to remember here is that if you said that the one-time offer is one-time only, you must stick with that. This means that next time you conduct a special offer or opportunity, your existing clients will know that when you say one-time, they'd better jump on the bandwagon now, or they'll miss out!

Week 52 –Run another transformation challenge. Use the before and afters from the first two and leverage the success of those events to pull in sponsors and publicity.

So there you have it – a full 12 month calendar to make sure you are maximizing your referral efforts. All you need to do is implement!

5 Proven Fitness Referral Strategies Guaranteed to Bring in Clients

As far as I'm concerned, referrals should be at the core of any good fitness pro's marketing system. The only problem is that using the same referral strategy over and over can get stale fast – so here are five ways you can keep the referrals coming in without sounding like a broken record.

Fitness Referral Strategy #1: Make it a Condition of Doing Business

Description: Make it a mandatory part of being your client. I know – it sounds easier said than done – but hear me out. This is especially effective if you have an in-demand service. State from the onset, as a condition of working with you, that clients each need to refer 2 friends. Obviously, you have to be tactful about it.

Here's an example of what you could say:

"If I do everything I've promised and you lose those 20 unwanted pounds, will you provide me with 2 referrals of friends, co-workers or family members that could use the same benefits?"

So, at the very beginning, your clients will know what they're in for.

Fitness Referral Strategy #2: Your Community's Best Businesses

Description: What you do is compile a list of other types of businesses that also serve your ideal client. After you've developed a comprehensive list of these types businesses, search through your database of clients, friends, and contacts for people that operate businesses in these categories. If there are business categories that you have no contacts with, look for a mutual friend that can serve as a liaison to a successful professional in that category.

Now, rank the professionals in each category as to which you'd prefer to affiliate yourself and your business with most. Send the "Tier 1" professionals a letter suggesting that you'd like to invite them to be a member of "Your Community's Best Businesses" and receive referrals from several of the other premier professionals in the community. Let them know that your goal is to create a network of the best local professionals in hopes of best serving each member's customers or clients and providing high quality referrals for the members.

This group would meet once a month and you would serve as the host/leader (another way of subtly enhancing your perception among group members). Each member would be able to present for 10-15 minutes as a means of educating the group about their business and how it would be of benefit to their customers/clients. Each member can make special offers to customers/clients of fellow group members, do endorsed mailings, etc. To increase the perception of this group, you launch a website (yourtownsbestbusinesses.com), do a newsletter, or provide testimonials from all of the happy, cross-referred customers.

This involves a little more work than most fitness referral strategies, but done well, it could easily provide you with more business than you could ever handle.

Fitness Referral Strategy #3: "Thank You" Gift Cards

Description: After a meaningful moment during a client's time with you – perhaps after they've met a goal or finished a 12-week program

– hand them 3 plastic gift cards and say, "Here are 3 gift cards that you can give to friends, co-workers, or family members that would like to enjoy the same results that you have. It entitles them to get $100 off our (name of program) program as a gift from you. And as a way of saying thank you for being such a great client I want to give you $X off of your next program as well."

Fitness Referral Strategy #4: "Thank You" Postcards

Description: Similar to the "Thank You" gift cards – after a meaningful moment during a client's time with you, hand them 2-3 pre-printed and stamped postcards that detail a special offer and say, "Here are 3 postcards that you can address to people important to you that you'd like to see benefit from changes similar to the ones you've made. It entitles them to get $50 off our (name of program) program as a gift from you. Simply address each postcard to someone important to you and sign them, and I'll be happy to put them in the mail. And as a way of saying thank you for being such a great client I want to give you $X off of your next program as well."

Both of these "thank you" strategies can be very powerful, but make sure that your client gets the credit for the gifts they give. If they don't get something out of giving the gifts, they're highly unlikely to give them. So when a gift card comes in, be sure to ask who provided the new prospect with the card.

Fitness Referral Strategy #5: Send a Gift To Work

Description: This is a great method to use, especially if your client has just graduated from a program you offer or achieved a specific goal. Send a big bouquet of balloons to your client's work congratulating them on their success. The balloons don't need to have any logo or writing on them…they just need to have a card congratulating the client on their success.

What will happen is that everyone at the client's place of work will ask who the balloons are from. The client will tell everyone about you and how much you've helped them. The balloons act as a talking point about how happy the client is with their trainer (you).

6

Mindset

Stop. Trying. Harder.

I remember my first couple of seasons as a college baseball coach.

Anytime we lost a game, I'd ramp up our practice efforts another notch. We'd go longer. Run more. Increase the intensity. My strategy was normal: "We'd just try harder."

But it wasn't working.

The increase in efforts offered little if any improvement.

Ironically, the struggle was part of the trap.

It was impossible for us to keep doing what we'd always done and make a massive shift in the results we were getting.

Trying harder doesn't always work.

Sometimes we need to do something radically different to achieve greater levels of success. We need to break out of our paradigm prisons, our habit patterns and our comfort zones.

No...I'm not suggesting you don't need to work hard. I love the Thomas Jefferson quote: "I'm a great believer in luck, and I find the harder I work the more I have of it."

But sometimes working harder is not the right answer. Sometimes we need to work smarter.

If we are not getting the results we want, we may need to change what we are doing.

For me to design my Ideal Business I had to make a massive shift and sell a business I'd built for a decade and approach things in a truly different way.

For Justin Yule, it was redesigning his business that allowed him to double revenues almost instantly.

For BJ & Kori Bliffert it was stripping away all the unnecessary that allowed them to see a 40% jump in just 10 weeks.

I could go on and on...but you get the picture.

You can't do what you've always done…even if you work a little harder doing it…and expect massively better results.

Not everything can be fixed with a hammer, no matter how hard you swing. Sometimes you need a different tool.

But here's the good news…

…instead of settling for small increases in your revenue, personal income or freedom…you can see massive leaps by approaching things in a different, smarter way.

The only real question is this:

Are you willing to change your actions and your approach enough to change your results?

Make This Switch for Success

You're probably more capable than you've ever imagined - but you have to let go of the artificial restraints.

You can create your Ideal Business - and reap all the rewards that it yields - through repeated, focused effort...but you can't do it if you tell yourself it's impossible.

You can't do it if you lock yourself in your own prison of doubt.

You have to be willing to make a trade if you're going to be successful.

You've got to be willing to trade *'I can't because...'*

And in return for giving that up you must embrace *'How will I...'*

See, I'm of the belief that you can largely do what you think you can do...and you cannot do what you think you cannot do.

Yes, there are exceptions...but more often than not, that's the case.

Now understand that by making this trade - you'll be giving up that addiction to excuses and reasons that you've likely been groomed to have over a lifetime...the fine art of rationalizing that most of us have been brought up with.

Instead, you're simply going to get the job done and achieve your goals.

No more making every excuse in the book and having others sympathize with you while underneath knowing that you settled for less than you deserved.

By making this trade you're now going to go and get what it is that you truly want.

You're going to start disregarding negative advice and instead seek out those who know 'how to' achieve what it is that you want to achieve.

Forget the people who tell you it can't be done and instead simply do it.

I assure you that if you're willing to set a target, then work smart and work hard...you'll get there.

And if you borrow the expertise of someone who has already been there...well, then you'll likely arrive twice as fast.

So the question is this: Are you willing to make the trade?

Secret To Achievement?

I've spent more than my share of time around both people who struggled to achieve much success in life and people who enjoyed one success after another.

I grew up in a small, poverty stricken town that fell on hard times after the local steel mill closed (at one time the town actually had an NFL team...) and thousands of jobs disappeared.

I also have worked with probably more fitness professionals personally than anyone on the planet when it comes to growing a business.

And I've enjoyed spending time around hundreds of millionaires and top achievers from dozens of different fields.

So the diversity of people I've spent my time around is vast...and I think the difference in achievement from the ordinary to the extraordinary largely centers around one thing:

The way someone thinks.

Not how intelligent they are or how talented.

One of the smartest guys I knew (and my freshman roommate in college) later died from an overdose...and while he was an extreme case, I know plenty of broke 'geniuses'.

I've seen literally hundreds of talented people struggle to achieve much of anything.

No - I'm talking about how you think about achievement.

That you think that not only is success possible...but that you've got what it takes to achieve it, you deserve it and that you're going to make it happen.

That you think bigger than the average person.

When most people are thinking that 'the normal' they see around them is their ceiling - you're thinking that you're capable of so much more.

When others blame the economy or circumstances - you know that you control your own economy.

You simply have to decide what you want, believe you deserve it and put yourself in a situation to make it your reality.

It's really that simple.

So think big...but be specific. If you want to draw your map, you need a precise destination.

Then do what you need to do to feel you deserve success. For me, the two things that helped me think that way were who I spent my time around and what I studied.

Then put yourself in a position to achieve it. That's the willingness to take strategic action.

I hope you really embrace what I've just shared...it can be the platform that your success is built on if you do.

One of the biggest mental shifts I have ever made when it came to making better decisions and ultimately working toward my Ideal Business was substituting one four letter word for another.

Instead if thinking: 'Should I spend my time doing this?', I switched to thinking...

'Should I spend my life doing this?'

See, sometimes I think that the way we think about things or talk about things is designed to minimize the impact of our choices.

If I say that I spend 50% of my time dealing with stuff in my business that I didn't particularly enjoy...I could rationalize it as the cost of doing business or tell myself that most people spend far more time than that doing things they don't enjoy.

But if I say I spend 50% of my life in that same situation - it seems far more troubling. I'm more motivated to change because I can't retrieve that 50% of my life once it's gone.

Maybe it's just semantics...but the way we spend our time is actually the way we're spending our lives...and to me that means no settling.

When I really embraced this way of thinking I knew that creating my Ideal Business wasn't just an interesting idea...it was a must.

My belief is that when you decide what and who you're spending your time on...you shouldn't settle - because you're actually spending your life on them.

So whether you choose to use this approach or not, the message is really that you have the opportunity to do, be and have almost anything you want...but you can't achieve any of it by settling.

And every day that you're not pursuing your Ideal Business, spending time with those that are important to you or doing the things that you truly want to do is a day you can't get back.

We all have the same 168 hours each week...are you spending yours the way you want?

Avoid This Person At All Costs…

The Dream Killer.

They're everywhere and they're trying to force you to settle for mediocrity the same way that they have.

They're going to tell you not to follow your dreams.

They're the people telling you that you can't build your Ideal Business.

That your clients will never have the body that they want.

You remember the movie *Rudy*?

Why is it still popular 22 years after it was released?

Because Rudy achieved his dream against all odds and in spite of being surrounded by Dream Killers.

A father who told him to settle for working in the mill.

A brother who never achieved his potential and now wanted to saddle Rudy with the same fate.

A teacher who said he wasn't good enough.

But he believed and persevered…and ultimately achieved his dream.

We love that story because we all can relate to that story…and we all have Dreams.

We've all had experiences with Dream Killers…I know I have.

I grew up in a small town where thinking big was getting a job that paid $30,000 a year.

I had plenty of people in my life telling me to settle for graduating and getting a 'stable job.'

In fact, I'd say that I could count the number of people who believed in my Dream of being a successful college baseball coach on one hand.

Then, when I went into business…same thing… 'You're a coach…not a business owner.'

So why are dream killers this way?

Fear.

Envy.

Jealously.

Ignorance.

Not all of them have bad intentions. Some have had negative experiences in their own lives and they might just be trying to protect you from the same.

But more often than not, they just have the Crab Bucket Mentality.

Have you heard the Story of the Crab Bucket?

One time a man was walking along the beach and saw another man fishing in the surf with a bait bucket beside him. As he drew closer, he saw that the bait bucket had no lid and had live crabs inside.

"Why don't you cover your bait bucket so the crabs won't escape?" he said.

"You don't understand," the man replied, "If there is one crab in the bucket it would surely crawl out very quickly.

However, when there are many crabs in the bucket, if one tries to crawl up the side, the others grab hold of it and pull it back down so that it will share the same fate as the rest of them."

Your Dream Killers are pulling you back down so that you settle for sharing the same fate as them.

Now those Dream Killers will try to justify why you or your clients should settle for mediocrity just as they have…

'You're just big boned.'

'You look good just like you are.'

'No one actually builds their Ideal Business, it's just a fantasy.'

But this is your chance to be the coach that your clients need…the person encouraging their dreams and then providing the plan, the coaching and support they need to make them a reality.

And that's what I want to do for you.

See, while there will be countless Dream Killers in your clients' lives and in your life as well…it only takes one person to help them believe that they can make their Dream a reality…and that person is you.

You're the coach that can provide the path to getting them where they want to go, around all the roadblocks others try to put in their way.

So if you've ever let the Dream Killers drag you down…don't despair. We all have.

But it's not a death sentence.

If you still have the Dream of Building Your Ideal Business…you can do it…just as your clients may have struggled until they found you, where their goal finally could become a reality.

But you have to believe you can.

Because when you truly do…you can spot those Dream Killers a mile away and avoid them dragging you down into their bucket of mediocrity.

You Decide

I just have one lesson I hope you'll truly embrace because it can not only transform your business, but it will also change your life:

You Decide.

We each are granted a finite number of years to do with what we want, but all too often we let fear or a lack of confidence or even naysayers prevent us from pursuing what we want.

Well, I'm here to tell you that if you want something and you're willing to do the things it takes to have it…in more cases than you can probably imagine, you'll succeed.

Yes, if you're 5'8" you're probably not going to play in the NBA or if you're reading this now and thinking *'well I always wanted to be President'*…the odds are not in your favor…but with so many things, your success simply boils down to you deciding to *go get it.*

It's now been 20 years, but it's as fresh in my mind as if it happened yesterday.

The Head Baseball Coaching position came open at my alma mater, where I'd been an assistant coach the previous season. It was a relatively new program that had only employed 2 previous coaches, and in spite of each having great resumes neither coach had ever enjoyed any success there…not a single winning season.

So when I wanted to apply for the job, few if any thought I had a chance to get it and the number of people who thought I'd succeed once I did get the job (I was the youngest college coach in the country for 2 years) I could count them on 1 hand.

If those other guys…a former Major League All-Star and a Hall of Fame Coach couldn't win, how could I? I heard it from literally dozens, if not hundreds of people…people essentially looking me in the eye and saying 'you're going to fail'.

We had a winning record the first season and won every season thereafter…becoming a nationally successful program and even finishing 5th at the World Series…the best finish from any team in our conference's history.

Now were those people just being mean? Were they intentionally trying to undermine my confidence?

Nah. They had their own opinions, experiences and fears…and they were projecting them on to me.

But they each get to Decide what they want to do with their lives (or not do) and **so do we**.

And their failures, fears or missed opportunities should never hold me or you back from what we want to achieve.

When I wanted to own my own business, I heard it all again…

You're a coach. You should be coaching baseball. That's what you were meant to do.

(Ironically, many of the people who were telling me I was going to suck as a baseball coach previously were actually saying this.)

But they've never owned or succeeded in business. They saw their world from their view…not mine.

Then I heard it one more time when we decided to move away from an offline business as the core of what we did to an online one being the core business.

Most people didn't understand it so they immediately tried to start shooting it down.

Again – not being mean or malicious…they were viewing things from their perspective.

But, by that point, I *knew* that *I Decide.*

I even saw it coaching Tyler's baseball team.

For 2 years I was an assistant coach for Tyler's baseball team. This season our coaching staff decided that we would start another team to create opportunities for kids who wouldn't have made that team.

I volunteered to take the 'B' team. So when tryouts happened, the 'A' team chose their roster (minus Tyler) and I took what was left over. Well, our 'B' team played the 'A' team twice.

We won both times.

Those kids decided that they were not going to let someone else tell them they weren't as good as the other players.

Now I know…all of this sounds cliché. It's all stuff you've heard before.

But in the role I play with now thousands of fitness professionals, you wouldn't believe the cool success stories I get to see. They're often really amazing.

And in so many of those cases, the person achieving such great things simply decided to go make their dreams or goals happen…in spite of long odds or naysayers or even personal fears.

They wanted to do something BIG. Something significant. And they did.

Really, that's one of those things that has driven me at times. Not wanting the ordinary.

I remember after leaving coaching I was offered a couple jobs in pharmaceutical sales. They each paid about twice what I'd been making as a coach.

But I asked myself this: *When I retire, will I really be satisfied looking back and saying that's what I did with my professional life? Will I be proud? Will I have something extraordinary to share with my grandkids? Or will I have just settled because that's what 99% of society does?*

I decided: No settling. Ever.

Even though turning that baseball program around was a relatively small achievement in the scheme of things…it allowed me to know that if you're willing to do what most won't…you can accomplish a lot of things they – and maybe even you – don't think are possible.

You just have to **Decide**.

So decide what you want and go get it.

The 1st Step to Success

A journey of a thousand miles begins with a single step.
~Lao-tzu

Do you have a goal that you want to pursue?

Are you finding it difficult to take that first step toward making this goal a reality?

What's holding you back?

What has stopped you from taking those first steps to success?

Here are a few that have affected me at one time or another in the past:

Feeling Overwhelmed. Read the Lao Tzu quote again: 'A journey of a thousand miles begins with a single step.'

No matter how large or how small the endeavor, you still have to begin with a single action. You don't have to have it all figured out. Simply take the first step.

Fear of _____. (Fill in the blank.) It could be any number of things.

Failure. Humiliation. Loss.

Odds are the fear that you're experiencing is far worse than the actual reality, if whatever you're afraid of did happen. 99% of the time, the fear that's holding you back is not that big of a deal. The potential discomfort you'd experience is nothing compared to the elation you'd experience from actually achieving your goal.

Unwilling to Leave The Comfort Zone. This is just a nicer way of saying you're being too lazy to reach your goals.

You must accept that achieving anything of significance requires work and dedication. So log out of Facebook, quit texting and hop off the couch and make your dreams happen.

Comparing Yourself with Others. Your objectives should simply be tied to reaching your own potential.

Don't worry about other people and what they've done unless it fuels you to work harder and do more. Otherwise focus on being the best version of you.

Thinking Things Had to Be Perfect. Waiting until the situation is perfect is a direct route to inaction because the situation will never be perfect.

No matter how well prepared you are, there will always be something unexpected that pops up, so don't let the need for perfection stand in your way.

Doing More Research. This is just another way of saying 'you're too lazy to do the real work.'

As I just mentioned, things don't have to be perfect to get started, so the need for endless research before taking action is completely unfounded.

Not Feeling 'Worthy' Enough. Not believing that you had enough education, knowledge, skill or experience can stop you before you get started, but the truth is that you can't get experience without 'doing' and you can't develop your skill without practice.

Most every 'expert' I know felt this way at one point or another and still proceeded to take action. So should you.

If you're like me, the six things that I listed above have at one time or another stood between inaction and action. But they're all just small obstacles designed to separate the haves from the have-nots. The successful from the average. The real bottom line is this: no matter what your goal is, the best time to start is now.

I learned this back when I became a college baseball coach at the ripe old age of 23. At that point I was the youngest collegiate head coach in the country and felt a version of all seven things I listed previously:

Becoming a head coach was completely overwhelming for someone who'd just graduated college a few months before. Being responsible for over 30 young men and a collegiate athletic program was far more responsibility than I'd ever had before.

I was afraid of failure and humiliation. The program had never had a winning season prior to my taking over in spite of being led by two well-known and previously successful coaches, so the odds were stacked against me and I was worried about doing so poorly that I'd be fired and ruin any chance of getting another job in coaching.

It's easy to say, 'I'd like to be a college coach' but actually stepping up and applying and potentially being rejected was something that I struggled with.

I looked at all the coaches of the programs I'd be coaching against and it was obvious that they were far more experienced, more knowledgeable and had superior resources. I also took notice of the two previous coaches who'd held the position that I was applying for and recognized that by most any standard they were far superior to me as a coach.

I knew that the circumstances I was potentially entering were not ideal. A program with poor resources, a limited budget and no track record of success wasn't exactly the ideal launching pad for a successful career.

Most 23-year-olds that were interested in being a baseball coach were taking positions as Assistant Coaches for High School JV Teams, not going after Collegiate Head Coaching jobs. Why should I be any different?

But, ultimately, I accepted the premise above: the best time to start is now.

And I learned as I went.

When I started coaching, I didn't know how to run a practice, how to motivate players or how to recruit effectively.

But I accepted the challenge and started the job anyway.

The first few months were really tough.

After my first season I still hadn't 'found myself' as a coach.

We had a winning season (barely), the first in school history in my first year, but it was more of a throwing-stuff-against-the-wall-to-see-what-sticks approach than actually figuring things out.

Thankfully, the experience taught me a lot. The next year the team did better. By the third season we were nationally ranked, and in the fifth season we finished fifth at the World Series.

And none of this would have happened unless I took the first step in spite of my insecurities.

And what I learned through that experience has benefited me time and time again.

No matter what your goal, success is a process and it requires overcoming limiting beliefs and taking action.

Maybe your goal is to finally start your business.

Perhaps it's to launch a Virtual 2nd Location online.

Maybe your goals are to get to $500,000 in business revenue or $100,000 in personal income.

It really doesn't matter whether you want to start a business or grow one. Whether you want to create your first info-product or turn your product into a half-million dollars a year business.

Actually, I'd encourage you to dream big and set lofty goals for yourself. That's part of what makes life worth living.

But you must understand, the key isn't so much what the goal is, but how you act on it.

Once you've set your goal, big or small, you will do much, much better if you spend more time thinking about your 'first steps' than just the big picture dreams and goals that you've laid out.

Just recently while doing a coaching session with a client of mine, I suggested that in addition to the big dreams he had set out for himself, I wondered if he might also benefit from having some realistic goals for the short term.

I then proceeded to suggest a few.

While I don't know your particular 'big goals', here are a few example first step goals that will help you generate momentum and start making real progress toward where you want to be:

If you want to launch a product, consider setting a filming date and hiring a videographer.

If you want to grow your business by 100 clients this year, start with adding two next week.

If you want to take 100 days off next year, start by scheduling a vacation or at least a long weekend.

If you want to go from a personal income of $40,000 /yr to $100,000 /yr, commit to adding $500 in monthly income in February.

To someone who is where you want to go, these kinds of goals might seem rather small and insignificant – but to get the momentum you need to succeed they'd be a good start.

To get to your big dreams there are a lot of steps in between.

And many of those steps might not be as exciting or as fun to think about as the big endpoint you've identified as your ideal destination. But often it's important to focus on the very next steps that you need to take in order to move towards your goals.

This is how you generate momentum.

By putting one foot in front of the other.

By getting one new client.

By writing a newsletter to your subscribers when taking an hour to check Facebook sounds far better.

Success isn't a big leap.

It's the combination of hundreds or even thousands of little steps in succession.

But most people don't recognize that, so they look for the magic bullet.

The quick fix.

And while this isn't good news if you're looking for immediate gratification, it's great news if you're willing to start stepping.

Because you understand that the magic is in the process and the process begins with that first step.

And don't think that you're stuck taking what you may feel are baby steps for long. Once you've achieved these first small goals, start to increase them.

You might want to go from taking that long weekend to a full vacation or from adding $500 in monthly income to $1000.

Before you know it, you've put a series of steps together and you're well on your way to achieving your big goal.

But before you can run, you need to walk.

So to quote Dr. Denis Waitley – "There never was a winner who was not first a beginner."

The most important thing you can do to make your goals a reality is that first step.

What is Your Story?

What stories do you tell yourself?

What stories do you tell yourself concerning your disappointments and failures?

Do you tell yourself that you were a victim?

Do you question whether you are destined for success?

Or do you say to yourself that they're lessons on the way to success.

Do you tell yourself that you're bad at sales? That you don't like 'the business side' of owning a business?

Are you telling yourself a story where you can't build the business that you want…that this sort of success is for 'lucky, special or different' people?

Perhaps it's time you start telling different versions of those stories.

The stories you tell yourself are the foundations of your self-image…and that self-image is the bedrock your success is and will always be built on.

If your story reveals you to be a victim, as unlucky or as short of the tools needed for greatness…you become an obstacle to your own success.

But if the story you tell yourself presents you to be resilient, resourceful, smart and strong…then those obstacles and challenges you face are the battles you have to fight to achieve your ultimate success.

It's all a matter of perspective.

A wonderful way to think about this can be derived from this powerful quote…

"Every day is a new opportunity to change your life. You have the power to say 'This is not how my story ends.'"

It says that you get to be the author of that story you tell yourself.

You just have to decide how you want your story to read.

Do you believe that you can succeed? That you can accomplish great things?

I hope you do…and I hope that's the story you're telling yourself, because the story in your head will often precede the reality that you achieve.

So author wisely.

The 1 Key Trait for Success

Decades ago Napoleon Hill interviewed hundreds of successful entrepreneurs.

His works like *Think & Grow Rich* are legendary - and his influence has been felt by millions.

But one of his most important findings, in my opinion, was that of all the successful people he interviewed, there was only one common personality trait shared by all.

The single trait that so many successful people had in common wasn't superior intelligence.

Sure many were quite smart…but others had only ordinary intellect.

It wasn't an extroverted personality.

It wasn't a particular type of scholastic background or being born into money.

The one trait that all the successful entrepreneurs Napoleon Hill shared was decisiveness.

They all were willing to make decisions and take the responsibility that came with them.

This finding isn't unique.

One of the two most important business books I've ever read is titled *Ready, Fire, Aim*…again, implying that you need to decide. You need to act.

See - we all know that you have to take action to succeed…but action is preceded by a decision. And most people are content to sit on the fence and not make decisions…important decisions that can dramatically improve their businesses and even their lives.

We fear making a decision. We fear that by deciding to take one path we will miss out on what's down the other.

We fear that by deciding to do something new we might fail.

But make no mistake…every day your future is being decided for you…either by you or by someone else.

And let me tell you a little secret about making decisions…

…sometimes you'll be wrong. Sometimes you'll have a bit of regret.

And that's ok…because no one gets it right 100% of the time.

I've been in leadership roles for over 20 years, making dozens of decisions daily…from who to recruit or when to change pitchers as a coach (I still screw that one up all the time) to what to write about or even something big like launching PatRigsby.com a while back.

And I've gotten a bunch of those decisions wrong.

But when it came to the big decisions…my only regret was not making them a little sooner.

See - success belongs to the bold.

Those who are willing to lead. Those who are willing to take action.

Those who are willing to decide.

Rarely does someone who constantly procrastinates or simply waits to be told what to do make it big.

So if you want to build your Ideal Business…decide.

If you want to finally create a virtual 2nd location…decide.

I don't mean simply saying it's going to happen someday.

Decide that today is the day that you begin.

That's how all big achievements begin. Are you ready for yours?

My Plan for Dealing with FEAR

A while back, I had 3 successive conversations with people about fear and overcoming adversity.

People who feared they might fail.

People who'd been knocked down…or knocked themselves down.

And what I know is that they're not unique.

They're not alone.

We've all got our fears.

We've all had our challenges and our struggles.

I know I have.

I've had 3 separate points in my adult life where I feared that I might fail.

Where an adversity I'd experienced made me question myself.

Here's how I overcame those points…

1. I reflected back on the success I'd had to that point. What I had achieved and how I got there. That it was earned and deserved.

2. I took the time to acknowledge that fear was a natural, impulsive

response, but the acronym that seems like a cliché is in fact true.

False

Evidence

Appearing

Real

I looked back at those successes I'd had and that was real...while my fears were based on hypotheticals. So, I accepted that while it was okay to have some fear of the unknown, I had earned the right to be confident in myself.

3. I stacked up small wins. If you want confidence, the easiest way to get it is to experience success...so instead of the natural reactions to fear of freezing or overthinking things, I found ways to achieve small victories that would give me the confidence and momentum I needed.

4. I strengthened the environment...what I was reading, who I was talking to or spending time with...each time I purposefully put myself in an environment that would lift me up, motivate me and push me to succeed. That's part of why I love reading and love Mastermind groups the way that I do...beyond the education we get from them, they help us create an environment for us to thrive.

So that's how I've dealt with my fears. And while I can't promise you that it will yield the same results for you that it has for me...I'd be willing to say that I'm certain that it would help.

Just don't beat yourself up over your failures or challenges. Don't let your fears get the best of you.

We all have them…it's part of the process. It's part of life.

Stay the course toward where you want to go…and use this (or your own variation) as a tool to help you on the journey. You're going to face these things along the way and your ability to get through them and overcome your fears is what will allow you to achieve the things you want to while others allow themselves to get derailed or settle for less.

7

Thoughts and Tips

Lessons I Learned From Competitive Athletics

Where did you learn what it takes to be successful?

For me – outside of what my parents taught me – competitive sports had by far the biggest impact.

It's funny, thinking back to the things I learned in high school, as an undergrad, and in graduate school – not a lot of it has a daily impact on what I do.

But the lessons I learned in sports – they matter every day.

Here are a few of the things being an athlete or coaching athletes taught me:

- **The Ability To Handle Adversity** – You can't go very far as an athlete without having to overcome adversity, and the most successful athletes are usually the ones who deal with adversity the most effectively.

- **Work Ethic** – I remember my freshman year of high school going to baseball practice at 3:15 after school and being done at 8. It was kind of a rude awakening for a 14-year-old, but I quickly learned that to be successful you couldn't do just enough to get by. I don't know anyone who has ever become a real success just punching the clock and working 9-5.

- **The Intangibles Matter As Much As The Tangibles** – Many of the most talented athletes I've ever played with or coached were huge underachievers when it came to performance. They didn't have the passion, drive, or willingness to work hard. They couldn't handle adversity. To this day – I'll hire intangibles 10 times out of 10 over a great resume.

- **To Keep Score** – The beauty of sports is that you keep score. There is a tangible way to measure performance. I tracked everything as a coach because I was looking for an edge. We track our numbers for the same reasons now; if you don't keep score, you cannot measure how you're performing and know where to focus your efforts on improvement.

- **Sacrifice & A Team Attitude** – If you compete in a team sport and want to succeed at a high level, you quickly learn to work within the framework of a group, sacrifice some of your individual goals for the good of the team, and understand that if you want to be a champion you need to get past selfishness and shortsightedness.

- **You Can't Hide** – In baseball, when you step in the batter's box it's a moment of truth. You either put in the hours or you didn't. As a coach, when your team takes the field, you either recruited and did the job preparing your team, or you didn't. Too many people make excuses. Sports teach you that excuses don't get you very far.

- **Hustle Can Make Up For A Lot** – As a player I got to play at a higher level than my talent probably would have taken me because I worked hard. As a coach we developed a nationally ranked program with some of the worst resources in the country. If you're willing to outwork the competition, you will be able to overcome a lot of shortcomings – whether it is talent, resources, or anything else.

That's just a sample of the things being involved in competitive athletics taught me. If you were involved in sports – what did they teach you?

Final Thoughts

- **Act on what you learn.** Knowing what to do and not doing it is the same as not knowing what to do.
- **It doesn't matter what you know.** It matters what you apply. If you don't apply something it's wasted knowledge.
- **Clarity is the precursor to success.** Get clear about what you want...be specific. If you know what you want everything else becomes easier. Decisions are clear. Motivation is constant. The path gets more defined. I promise it's not 250K in gross revenue or 150 clients. It's what you think attaining those things would yield. Do you want a personal income of 100K, to take 2 weeks of vacation

a year, not to work Saturdays or be in the gym from 5 a.m. until 9 p.m? You decide what you want – then go get it.

- **Know what you need & get it**. Every successful training business needs to have certain processes in place. First you need to know what those processes are – then you need to get them in place in your business. Burying your head or procrastinating on this will prevent you from ever having your Ideal Business.

- **Know who you are** and who you're really trying to serve.

- **You decide.** You decide how people view you and your business, along with what hours you'll work and how you live your life. If you don't decide, they'll decide for you.

- **Fixing your business starts with fixing you.** You need to work on you as much as you work on your business. You're the engine so if you're not functioning at a high level then you can't expect your business to.

- **Decide what you want to be known for and share it.** If you want to build a great business you need to have an identity…your clients need to be able to talk about you and clearly share why you're awesome. Can they?

- **Are you the first person in your market that people think of?** If not, get better, re-define what you do, or tighten down your niche.

- **Best beats first.** Be so good at what you do that no one else in the world can do what you do. You may not have been the first in your market but it doesn't matter as long as you commit to being the best.

- **There is always room for someone to come in and be great.** The market never needs more average providers.

- **Your opportunity.** I only had a couple great college professors, and one of them really stood out. He told me that you can become a millionaire by doing anything, as long as you're willing to be better than everyone else at it. I agree 100%, but most people won't do what it takes to be better than everyone else.

- **If you want a business and a life that only a select few have**...you've got to be willing to do what few are willing to do.
- **Passion + production = performance.**
- **"I'll try" really means "I'm not really committed and this probably won't happen."**
- **If you want to build a great business solve other people's problems.** People will pay more money to for you to make their life easier.
- **Make sure the reality of what you're selling is as good or better than the marketed perception of it.**
- **Be the best you**...not the best imitation of someone else.
- **Avoid Average** – The average business owner starts a business because they hate their current job and want to do something they think they like to pay the bills. This is average. Don't be average. Hating your job is no better of a reason to start a business than disliking your current significant other is for marrying someone you don't know. If you want to build a great business you're passionate about, then build something great because you have a passion for what you do. Those types of thoughts should drive you... not avoiding a job you hate.
- **Be remarkable.** No one raves about ordinary. Deliver an extraordinary experience and a caliber of service that people can't help but talk about, and everything else about business becomes much, much easier.
- **My favorite personal times are simple family 'hang outs'** like Holly, Tyler, Alex and I watching a ballgame or just playing at home. Nothing beats low hassle quality family time.

- **My favorite business times are our Mastermind Meetings.** Nothing beats being around a group of like-minded, motivated fellow entrepreneurs. Do it at least a couple times per year.
- **Associate with like-minded, successful people.** It's often said that you're the average of the five people you associate with the most. I don't know if 5 is the magic number but the concept is spot on, so don't hang out with slackers.
- **Model other people's success.** Learn from people that have enjoyed successes similar to the ones you want. Model what they've done to get where they are.
- **Practical vs. Formal Education.** There is a much stronger correlation between your practical education - stuff like Perform Better events, business coaching, etc. - and your professional success than there is a relationship between your formal education and your professional success.
- **Never stop learning.** At every seminar I've ever been to, the most successful people always seemed to be asking questions and taking notes. This is not an accident.
- **Invest in yourself if you want to grow.** Investing in you is better than any stock you can buy. I've invested in my education in the past year more than ever before - and my new business doubled my expectations.
- **Education Is An Investment, Not An Expense** – *Every* single one of the top pros in the industry either benefit from Coaching or Masterminds. But they view education as an investment. If they invest $5000, they do it fully expecting to make 10X, 20X... maybe even 30 or 40X that back in return.
- **9 times out of 10 your biggest limiting factor is in your own mind.**

- **If you don't believe it can and will happen...it won't happen.**
- **Determine what you enjoy doing and do best - then outsource as much of the rest as possible.** For me that's writing, working with coaching clients and developing game plans for businesses and finding opportunities for growth are tops among my areas of focus.
- **If you want your problems solved - start looking for solutions.** Don't dwell on the problems.
- **Successful people implement stuff in a hurry.** Procrastination is not acceptable. The faster your speed of implementation - the bigger your bank account.
- **Successful people are always growing.** Success is never stagnant.
- **Think BIG** – The most successful trainers and coaches I know all think differently than the rest. They all think much bigger. They think about doing big things, not ordinary things. They set big goals. They take big actions. Big achievements don't begin with little dreams.
- **Stay One Step Ahead** – The fitness pros who are growing a training business to the highest level are relentless in their quest to improve. There is zero complacency. They're always improving. Always looking for another edge. Staying the same isn't ever a consideration.
- **High achievers aren't smarter or more talented**...they just do the things everyone else just dreams about doing.
- **Focus on behaviors rather than outcomes.** You can control behaviors and by disciplining yourself to enforce the new habits you'll almost always assure yourself of getting the outcome you want.
- **Learn by 'doing' - not by talking about it.** If you want to get good at public speaking...speak. Want to get good at

writing...write. Want to become a better salesperson...get in front of more people and sell.

- **The first couple weeks of doing something outside of your comfort zone are always the hardest.** Discipline yourself to get through that and you'll typically be able to stay the course. For me, writing was like pulling teeth in the beginning. Now it's one of my favorite things.

- **Business is like fitness.** There is no magic pill and results don't come overnight. Focus on the process and you'll get there and enjoy the journey.

- **Do the same thing you've always done and you'll get the same thing you've always gotten.** The people I've enjoyed watching achieve tremendous growth all stepped out of their comfort zone to get there.

- **It never has changed and never will:** You can't help people until they want to help themselves.

- **The grass isn't greener on the other side.** The grass only gets greener if you water it.

- **Life isn't always fair.** Accept it and move on to making the most of the hand you're dealt.

- **Luck does happen...people do get lucky.** And you're a lot more likely to 'get lucky' if you put yourself in the right spot for luck to happen. Even the people who win the lottery at least bought a ticket.

- **It's never too late to start following your dreams.**

- **Double down on your strengths.** Better to be great at a few things than average at many. Specialist > Generalist.

- **Build around those strengths.** Hire to compliment them. Streamline, automate or eliminate / minimize the areas you're weak. You probably can't eliminate the role your weaknesses have in your business…but you can minimize them.

- **You're not too busy**. We choose how to spend our time. You just decided something else was more important. I do it all the time. I choose to go play with Alex instead of answering emails or doing other stuff.
- **Organize your day the night before.** Block time for everything that is important to you. Working on your business gets time. Networking gets time. Family gets time. Self-improvement gets time. If you don't schedule it, you'll find yourself putting it off.
- **Don't leave the day to chance.** If you don't plan out what you need to accomplish you'll likely be allowing everyone else to decide how you spend your time. Not good.
- **Set deadlines for everything.** Deadlines are the difference between getting stuff done and just talking about it. If you treat every work day like you're going on vacation tomorrow, imagine how productive you'd be.
- **Get 2-3 Drivers / Rocks Done each day**. You'll probably have a long to do list most days…but 2-3 things will be drivers that can really move you forward…don't let the other stuff prevent you from doing those.
- **There are not enough Producers**. There are too many people who spend their time reacting and not enough time producing the results that they want for themselves and for others.
- **We need more coaching and less information**. A good plan executed is better than a great plan talked about. Make sure you're coaching the plan…not just giving it to them.
- **Coaching Is The Ultimate Accelerator**. Coaching provides a roadmap to follow and accountability to keep people on track. This is crucial for you to convey to your clients and is probably something you should keep in mind for yourself.
- **Simple is a good thing**. Don't overcomplicate things. Period.

- **Business owners deserve more than employees**. Yet most small business owners settle for a lot less than employees with the same number of years in their field.
- **Ideal Businesses are all around**. They're not necessarily what some people think of as lifestyle businesses…but businesses that allow the owners to enjoy truly satisfying incomes, lifestyles that allow them to give ample time to the things that are important to them and provide a venue for them to reach their professional goals…that should be the expectation…not the exception.
- **There would be a lot more 6 figure earners in our industry**, if most people realized that they had all the same training skills (often better) as the top earning trainers in the field.
- **Opportunities are endless, but you can't act on them all at once.**
- **There is at least 10K hiding in every business.** Most people never look for it. Start by looking for it.
- **Tap into the hidden opportunities in your business.** It's money that's just sitting there waiting for you to grab it. But most people never take the time to look. Three easy ones are up-sells from your basic programs, more specialization and reactivation of previous clients.
- **Public speaking and webinars are underused tools.**
- **Offer strong guarantees.** The stronger the better.
- **Have an upsell for everything.** A minimum of 20% will take it.
- **Add down sells to convert more prospects.**
- **Make it easy to buy.**
- **Use EFT**… 95% of people pay things monthly.
- **Find ways to get people on recurring programs.**
- **Price is elastic**… have you checked how far yours can stretch?

- **Always have a higher priced option.** There are a certain percentage of people in every market who will pay top price.
- **It's not what you make, it's what you keep.** Focus on improving your net profits, not just your gross revenues.
- **Don't step over dollars to pick up pennies.**
- **A lot of success is born out of a hatred of losing.** As a coach I enjoyed winning, but I HATED losing. I think you need to enjoy it (success) to sustain it...but it often begins with hating the idea of failing.
- **Recognition and rewards are great motivators.** Use them often.
- **Business should be fun.** What don't I like about what I do? Being away from family when we're on the road, but other than that: nothing. Why do something that sucks? Enjoy your work, if you don't, find new work.
- **Scarcity creates action.**
- **People will pay more money to for you to make their life easier.** The more you can provide 'done for you' for your audience, the better off you'll be.
- **People are pretty predictable in what they'll buy.** Watch infomercials about fitness or fat loss. They want results fast. They buy based on emotion. Testimonials are more powerful than almost anything else you can share.
- **You can't be afraid to reinvent yourself.** Don't be afraid to transform your business model to better serve the market, to better position yourself against the competition, or to better apply what you've learned along the way to take advantage of a new or different opportunity.
- **There's power in creating a community.** If you can create a community, it will improve retention, generate referrals, and provide opportunities. Plus, it's just a more enjoyable environment to work in.

- **Not every offer needs to be accepted.** Just because it has some potential upside doesn't mean it's a good fit for you right now. There will always be people knocking, calling, emailing, and offering, and all of them will be asking you for your time. You don't have to answer the door, you don't need to answer the phone, and you don't need to respond to every email the minute it hits your inbox.
- **Handling adversity often is the difference between success or failure.** You will get knocked down. You will get humbled. What you do after that happens will determine how high you climb.
- **Focus on execution.** An idea by itself is almost always worthless. It's how you execute the idea that matters.
- **You only get paid for done.** The only things that matter are what you finish. One of the biggest reasons people fail is poor follow-through. They don't get things done. It doesn't take much to be an idea guy or start something.
- **Use surveys** to learn who your clients and prospects really are and what they really want.
- **One Is A Terrible Number** – If you're growing a training business, the number 'one' is your enemy. Having only one lead generation strategy. Having only one option to offer to prospective clients. Employing only one revenue stream. Being a one-person operation. All of them are potential roadblocks to success.
- **Success without work is a lie and doesn't happen EVER.** If you're starting out, assume that the path to beating the competition requires you to work harder and be better if you want to win.
- **If it's important, track it:** leads, FEOs, closed sales, retention. If you don't track it, you can't improve it.
- **The better the follow up, the better the business.**

- **Follow-ups matter.** I can count on one hand the number of times I've gotten a follow-up letter or card or call from anybody I've spent money with over the past year. It just never happens. And this was the best kind: thank you + sales pitch. There's a very simple formula for you. Send thank you cards and make an offer or ask for a referral.
- **Sizzle is fine in marketing, but education is better.**
- **You want better clients that refer more? Educate them.** The ones who "buy in" will become your biggest advocates.
- **Time is life.** We all have less of it today than we did yesterday. So quit wasting days doing things that aren't getting you closer to where you want to be. Otherwise, you'll look up and a decade will have passed, making it even harder to make big changes.
- **A big obstacle to success is distraction.** Turn off the email, Facebook and TV and work on your business.
- **"How do I get more clients?"** The answer is this: "Get one today. Get another tomorrow. Get another the day after that." That is the best answer no one wants to hear. They'd rather spend the next 3 months looking for a magic way to get 100 clients than simply get one a day for those same 3 months. Which do you think will work better?
- **You've got to be a little obsessive.** Growing a training business into your ideal business empire requires you to be a little obsessive about getting better each and every day. Most business owners don't do this. They essentially just go to work every day like they're an employee and not a business builder. If you want a great business, you need to get a little better every day – and that requires you to be somewhat obsessive about the details and improvement.

- **You have two jobs and two jobs only:** 1. Deliver a GREAT experience. 2. Make sure that EVERY DAY more people try your experience. Do those 2 things daily and you'll be all set.
- **Treat others the way you want to be treated.** That's the most important business advice you'll ever receive.
- **Treat everyone like a prospect.** Treat every prospect like a client. Treat every client like they're family. Treat your family (and business family) like gold. As far as I'm concerned, relationships are everything. Grow your relationships, and you'll also be growing your business.
- **Give to get.** If you treat people well, you'll be paid back 10X over.
- **A transaction is the beginning of a relationship, not the end of one.**
- **Relationship marketing trumps all other types of marketing.**
- **You get paid for relationships.** You are not just getting paid for the workout you provide. You are getting paid for the relationship the client has with you or feels they have with you and your business. Of course, with that relationship comes responsibility. You need to remember who's signing your paycheck, and what they are really paying you for.
- **Meet people where they are and sell them what they want.** Then give them what they need. This hold true in marketing where you need to be where your ideal prospects are located. It holds true in the service you provide, by being willing to adapt and customize the way you present what you offer to address the prospective client's wants and needs. It holds true in coaching where you need to adapt your solution to help people where they really are, not where you think they should be.
- **Live in their experience**. If you want to be more effective in

selling training or in growing your training business through maximizing the value of each client relationship, you've got to put yourself in their shoes. You need to know what keeps them up at night. You need to know what their day looks like. You need to speak their language. If you do this, being the best and most complete solution for them will become far, far easier.

- **Be a better listener** – If you want to sell more, listen more intently to what your prospects are saying. If you want to add revenue streams to your business, listen to what your clients are really asking for more help with. If you want to grow, listen to your network and they'll reveal a surprisingly large number of opportunities. If you really pay attention instead of just waiting to talk, business becomes much easier.
- **Improve the experience.** If you want to set yourself apart from every other fitness provider in your market, focus your efforts on delivering an extraordinary experience to your clients and prospects.
- **Success isn't hard:** you just have to find ways to organize, discipline, and motivate yourself to get more done, faster – not more started, more done.
- **Remember this Dan Kennedy phrase:** "Why should your prospect choose to do business with you vs. any and every other option available to them?"
- **Recycle what you do.** Deliver the same content in different formats.
- **Small hinges swing big doors.** A few small, but strategic changes like improving your closing percentage or adding an upsell at the point of sale can make big differences to your bottom line.
- **Find the void in a market** – then fill it.

- **Break out of the fitness industry norms** – the majority is almost always wrong and is always behind.
- **A different way to look at your market:** find price gaps instead of pricing the way everyone else does. If you can get a health club membership for $39, a bootcamp membership for $199, and 1 on 1 personal training for $500, then the gaps are $99 and $299-399. What can you offer there?
- **You can overcome a lack of money with an abundance of hustle in most areas.** Roll up your sleeves and go to work, knock on doors, hustle, network, and make something happen every day.
- **Mediocrity exists if you tolerate it.** If you accept mediocrity you will get more of it.
- **Help them help you.** People struggle with strategic alliances and referrals by not making it easy for others to help us. Do as much as possible of the work for them and you'll get 10X the results.
- **The quickest way to make more money?** Sell more to your current clients. Offer supplements, workshops, weight management, higher priced coaching, etc…
- **Get help.** Every day there are low return activities that you do and there are high return activities. Here's how I'd quantify each:

Low Return Activities:
- **Activities that could be outsourced for significantly less than your hourly worth.** If you can make $75 per hour training or can generate $1200 worth of new business public speaking, then you can certainly delegate $8 an hour work to free up your time.

- **Activities you don't enjoy at all.** If you really don't enjoy some facet of your personal training business, find someone who can do it effectively.
- **Activities you are bad at.** If you're bad on the phone, outsource Business of the Month calls & confirmation calls.

High Return Activities:
- **Activities that generate significant revenue, close to or exceeding your hourly worth.** Most marketing activities, sales, delivering service, program design, retention work, etc., falls in this category.
- **Activities you enjoy.** If you enjoy mowing your lawn, mow it. It doesn't really matter if you could earn more doing something else if it really makes you happy.
- **Activities you're best suited for.** If you're the best person at program design in your business or the best salesperson, those should be among the last things you delegate.
- **Delegate the lower skill activities first.** You don't have to spend a lot to start delegating. Offer a few hours to a client that would like to earn some extra money or train for free. Then your job is simple: You need to more than make up for the money you're spending delegating with the new time you've freed up.
- **You only get paid for done.** One of the biggest timewasters of all is not bearing down and finishing stuff, so until something's finished, it seems like time wasted. Luckily, the solution is simple: when you start a project, put the blinders on and finish it.
- **Offer a powerful guarantee.** At a minimum, 100% Money Back.

- **Have a powerful message that appeals to your ideal client.** If it doesn't make your ideal prospects jump up and say, "That's exactly what I want," then strengthen it.
- **Make it easy to buy.**
- **Have plenty of testimonials handy.** Social proof is crucial if you want to make selling easy.
- **Use a structured sales process.** If something works, stick with it.
- **Target better prospects.** That doesn't always mean more affluent prospects; target prospects that are a better fit for you and your business.
- **Give better service, all the time.** Every day you need to be on.
- **Under promise and Over deliver.**
- **Raise your rates.** You can do it in small increments, too. A $2 or $3 increase per session will get no resistance from clients but will add a lot to your bottom line over the year.
- **Treat everyone like you want to be treated.**
- **Start holding Transformation Contests** – at least 3 per year.
- **Run a buzz-worthy business.** If you run a great business, get clients incredible results, and have tons of energy, people will spread the word.
- **Do the most important thing first.** Nothing sets the tone for a productive day like knocking out a big task early.
- **Know when you work best.** For me early mornings, late evenings, and Sundays are best for writing.
- **Make it easy to get started.** Prep the night before, keep what you need handy, and eliminate distractions.
- **Use your time wisely.** We all have the same 24 hours each day, so why is there such a disparity in what high achievers

accomplish versus what the average person does? The answer lies in how they use those hours. Use yours wisely.

And lastly… Enjoy It! If you don't like your work, fix it!

8

Online

How to Launch a Product

A little while ago, I helped one of my former players launch his first InfoProduct.

I thought the overview of how this happened would be helpful to you when you're considering whether going online is right for you.

Here's the overview – step-by-step.

The Idea

I happened to be in Cleveland to attend a seminar, so I stopped over to see one of my former players, Brian Harrison, who was (and is) a coach at a local University.

He'd just led his team to the World Series and was really at the top of his game.

After talking for a bit we sat down and grabbed dinner…about then the conversation shifted from celebrating his successes to him expressing his frustration with the low ceiling of what he could earn in his current coaching job.

After 3 other jobs - where in each stop he was very successful – he'd finally been able to get a head coaching job at a good school that was just 5 minutes from where he grew up. He and his wife could raise their family in their hometown…but the drawback was that this sort of small college job would never pay the way that some of the premier Division One programs do.

He felt stuck.

We talked about various options and the conversation came up about him packaging up some of what he did so well as a coach and sharing it with others. The topic made for good conversation but I didn't think it would go anywhere. I was not really in a position to help much as I was about to start a long transition from my then current businesses into my own new business, and, well…I'd had that type of conversation with at least 250 other people with something valuable to share and who were excited about the possibility of creating their own product or online business that never went anywhere.

We talked every month or two and the topic kept coming up, but I didn't have much time to help…and truthfully, I thought it was mostly just talk.

Creating The Product

Then, close to a couple of months ago…actually on December 10th to be exact, he told me he'd filmed all the videos for a product and was going to try to get it to market. He was going to get some of the students at the University to put it together and he was going to try to write a sales page…and get this all done before he spoke at the biggest baseball convention in the country on January 9th.

We went to work turning this into a salable product…with the help of my team we had it ready to go on January 6th and it went live on January 7th.

Now, he didn't have his own list of subscribers or anything so we recorded the presentation he was going to give at the big Convention and gave it away as an opt-in gift and then wrote a very simple 3 email sequence promoting the product to anyone who opted in.

The Launch

Then he went to work getting the word out.

He texted all his coaching buddies and told them it was live…he had an assistant coach drive the 8-hour trip from Cleveland to Nashville and he texted or emailed people one at a time the entire trip.

He reached out to people he knew who had lists and asked them to share it with their audience. He leveraged every contact in his network.

By noon on the 8th he'd sold about $4900 worth of the product.

Then, he spoke to about 6500 coaches at the Convention on the 9th and got in front of an entirely new crowd – where he was able to tell them to go download the presentation at the opt-in page.

From there on, day after day it was $1000-$2000 in daily sales.

After 12 days the product was at $24,312 is sales. More than half his annual income from coaching.

As I write this 24-days after the launch, his total is over $29,000.

Things have slowed down a bit as he's been trying to manage the influx of communication, get started with some Facebook ads and as he gets into practices for the season ahead.

He's got a few more people ready to promote it, but now that he's not under the pressure of that deadline to have things ready for the speaking engagement he's stepping back to make sure he has everything in order. And maybe the best part is that this launch has created a platform which has already provided him with a number of new opportunities and will yield many more as he goes along.

So why am I sharing this with you?

A few reasons I guess…

First, I'm proud. He's the best hitter and one of the most enjoyable people I ever coached. Seeing how he's become an extraordinary coach over the past decade or so and now how he's sharing his expertise with the world is pretty awesome.

I'm biased, but I think he's the most innovative…and for my money, best hitting coach in the country. I think there are a number of people out there doing good work but I think he's got some incredible (and proven) expertise.

He deserves it. If you pour your heart and soul into something to become great at it…then you should be able to reap some financial reward from it. I don't think that you should have to compromise…be great at your craft or make money…be well paid or actually be able to spend time with your family…I don't think those things should be mutually exclusive.

And, really, I just wanted to show you how this actually works.

I don't think the world needs any more 'find a hot market' crap where marketers who don't have any subject matter expertise jump into a market and sell some ordinary (at best) product that is ghostwritten and it makes them a windfall of cash but leaves the customers worse off than before they bought.

I think it should work pretty much like it worked here.

Someone like Brian…and maybe like you…who has a passion for their craft and a proven expertise does great work with their own clients or their own athletes…

…then they decide to package that expertise up and start sharing it online.

Maybe they just create a single product and sell it to the people who are on their local email list and pick up a couple hundred additional dollars each month. Perhaps it's enough to pay for a vacation or to start putting a bit of money away for retirement.

Maybe they build it into a 2nd business…what I call the Virtual 2nd Location. We see some of the best in the industry have their facility and then also have a successful online business where they package up and share what they're doing. In many cases the Virtual 2nd Location becomes far more lucrative than the facility – but they still have the opportunity to actively coach, to keep learning and improving…and to often dial in who they're working with and their coaching schedule as it takes some of the financial driven pressure off.

Or maybe they're ready to get out of the in-person coaching business but still want to leverage the work they've been doing for years. I've run across people who are moving to a new town and don't want to start from scratch, coaches who've been coaching for 20+ years and are ready to step back a bit and try something new…or people who just want a bit more flexibility.

I know plenty of people that have built 7 figure online businesses and a number who've even created 8 figure ones…but they're the exception.

This, on the other hand, is the type of thing that I think is possible for anyone who has real expertise to share and is willing to do the work. Brian worked his butt off puting the product together…basically treating it like a 2nd job when it came to the creation of the product and the marketing during the launch. And it's an extension of work he's been doing for years…he's spent years building a strong network and honing his craft…and both have been leveraged heavily during this process.

But now he's made some real income…in this case already more than 50% of his annual salary. And he's still got orders coming in daily. My guess is that he'll do over 100K this year in gross sales. And perhaps the best part is that he's got a platform now…he can create other offerings, will have doors open to him and be in a position to make this a true, ongoing 2nd business if he chooses.

So if you want to create your own Virtual 2nd Location or simply launch your own product – this is a great blueprint to follow…one that is realistic, is built for a real coach who wants to grow and is reflective of the work involved and the potential upside.

Is This Holding You Back?

When I ask fitness entrepreneurs about their Ideal Business it often includes an online component.

Many either want to augment what they do locally with an online business like Mike Robertson, Eric Cressey, Mike Boyle, Alwyn Cosgrove,Todd Durkin and so many others have done.

-or -

They want to transition away from their local business as they get older and move primarily online.

Personally, I love the online component of business.

I don't think I could move away from doing live stuff as part of what I do...but the online piece has given me more flexibility and leverage than I could have ever imagined.

For my offline stuff, I do a lot of in-person consulting and Mastermind and am even considering the possibility of partnering in a sports performance business.

But in truth, despite the upside, the two reasons that most people don't add an online piece to their own business are these:

1. They won't invest enough time to get it off the ground.

2. They get overwhelmed because they forget that it functions almost exactly like an offline business.

So let's tackle the first obstacle...

Any expansion is going to take an investment of time. No exceptions.

If you see this as an expansion of your business instead of something different...you get that.

You wouldn't expect to go into a second location without investing money in equipment, spending time on buildout, getting marketing in place, selling new clients and making sure the service and experience were dialed in.

A pretty significant investment of time and money...and you're taking on a decent risk in signing a lease, coming up with the money for start-up and starting to spend your time away from your main location...all for what usually amounts to 25-30% profit if you're doing things really well.

With less time, money and risk you can start a business online to augment your main business and probably net more...but only if you treat it with the same focus you would a second location.

To me, the blend of lower risk and initial cost with the higher upside is a hard combination to pass up if you want to expand.

Now, as for that second obstacle...

Running an offline business and running an online business have far more similarities than differences.

You have to deliver a great solution that solves an important problem for someone.

You have to get people to know who you are and why you're the best option for them.

You have to be able to operate profitably.

Those are the core things that drive both your offline business and the online business.

So, packaging up what you're great at offline into an online solution...easy enough. Yes, it's different...but my businesses have done over 120 different products and I've coached people to create several times that many...I assure you that it's simple.

It's just different...for now.

Now the marketing...it's mostly the same concepts...you just have to consider two differences:

1. Instead of having geography as one of the things that differentiate you...that needs to be replaced with something else. A stronger hook, a smaller target market or a more unique position.

Right now you likely rely on a combination of being good at what you do, being somewhat different (but do prospects know why you're different?) and geography to attract clients...we just need to replace that last one with one of the 3 things I listed and you're in good shape.

2. We get lazy with marketing due to recurring revenue. Because people stay with us and keep paying we don't put as much effort into pursuing new clients. Online you need to do more with marketing...but it's not complex. Every other business but ours that doesn't have memberships has to do this...so I know you can.

Heck, I've hired both a plumber and a carpet cleaner in the past few months and both got over 90% of their leads online. Each was generating 75-100 customers a month.

If all you sold was a $47 product...do what they're doing and you're at $3525-$4700 per month...and neither of them were exactly internet gurus.

And as for the operating profitably...you're replacing a lease, equipment and trainers with a website or two, products and maybe some virtual or customer service help...being profitable online is simpler than offline if you deliver a good product and go get some customers.

So hopefully you see that this isn't as complicated as you might have made it.

9

Planning

3 Steps to Doubling Your Business

I know, I know...I'm making doubling your business sound way too easy, but stick with me here. I really think the key to you doubling your business is how you're investing your time.

Yes, investing, not spending.

Because if you're using your time as you should there will be a compounding effect...an effect far greater and one that will yield more ROI than any stock you're likely to buy.

So what are those 3 steps and how do they relate to investing your time?

Step #1: Planning how you're going to invest your day.

Each day someone is going to decide how your time is used.

The first key to doubling your business is to make sure that the first allocation of your time goes toward achieving the things that YOU want...because I can assure you that you're going to be helping someone achieve their goals each day - so it might as well be you.

How do you do that?

Well - here's the simplest approach:

Decide the top 2-3 things you need to do tomorrow to move you toward your goals - then make sure that you have time allocated to invest in those things. At the end of the day do a quick review on the progress you made, what you could do better and what your top 2-3 are for the next day.

Step #2: Move on to your weekly plan.

On the weekend, spend 15 minutes reviewing the previous week, looking at how you invested your time, celebrating your successes and mapping out what you want to accomplish to move your business forward in the next week.

This will set the stage for the daily planning that we touched on in the first step.

Step #3: Work ON your business.

So the third step is not the quarterly planning that you're probably expecting.

No - I'm a fan of yearly and quarterly planning and personally do both...but I think the thing that trumps both is taking time away to work ON your business.

That is step #3.

See - you could plan your upcoming quarter or even your upcoming year...but if you can't ever see the forest for the trees you miss out on the opportunity to truly craft a plan that will improve your business.

You're too immersed in the day to day to be creative, you can never get clear of what you're doing now to think about what is truly possible and how to get there.

I'll give you an example...I was at a meeting for the Mastermind Group I belong to and was able to work through mapping out four different projects I couldn't really ever get past sticking points and also figured out solutions to what I consider the 2 biggest challenges in my business.

In a day.

All because I could see things clearly...through the 'lens' of working ON my business rather than IN my business.

Now I can plug those things into my weekly and daily plans.

Now, it could be a coincidence that all that happened in my first work day away from my office...but I don't think it was.

So, there are the 3 steps to doubling your business.

Nothing magic about them...just being able to work ON what you want your Ideal Business to be and how to get there...then investing the time in making it a reality.

Not easy...but very simple.

So apply the 3 steps and get on the path to doubling your business.

This Destroys 95% of All Business Owners

I often have conversations with fitness business owners plagued by the same thing…

…the same disease that prevents at least 95% of fitness entrepreneurs from ever making real headway toward creating their Ideal Business.

The disease of Self-Inflicted Overwhelm.

To-Do Lists that seem to be never ending...but no real priorities.

Worry about things well beyond their control.

Chasing more information instead of executing things that are already proven to work.

Spending all their time thinking about the future, the past, the competition or anything else that prevents them from focusing on the present.

Avoidance of the activities that can be real game changes…instead spending their time reacting to low priority stuff or simply procrastinating.

Fear of everything that could go wrong.

You understand…and unless you're a cyborg you've probably fallen into this trap…I know I have.

And the reality is this…if you're spending too much time in this 'place' it's killing any chance you have of creating your Ideal Business.

So how do you cure it?

Well, here's my approach:

Step One: Get clear about your values and your priorities. Not some cliché stuff that you pulled off someone else's website…what's really important to you.

This is the filter all your decisions will go through…if something doesn't fit who you are and what you stand for…it doesn't get your time or attention.

Step Two: Decide where you want to go. Decide what success looks like to you. What your Ideal Business will be. This is the destination you're working toward from where you are today.

Step Three: Create your map and plan the first leg of the trip. Now the job is to create a map from where you are to where you want to be and then decide what you need to do during that first leg to make significant progress.

Now that first leg can be 100 days, 90 days, 12 weeks, 6 weeks or even a month. You decide.

I use 6 weeks for our Producer Challenge, but for a lot of my own planning I just use 3 month blocks…what can I realistically get done in 3 months?

Set your goals for what you'll do in your chosen time frame and you're all set.

Step Four: Weekly Planning

Now you just decide what you'll be doing each week to move you toward that goal so that you're on pace to accomplish it in the time frame you set (or sooner.) This is where people really start to get hung up though.

They may say they're going to get things done but they've not set aside enough time…or even any time…to do them. If you're like most fitness entrepreneurs, you'll schedule dozens of blocks to serve other people's goals…but never schedule one for your own.

If something matters, schedule it and give yourself enough time to do what you intend to do.

Step Five: Win The Day

Every day is a chance to make progress or lose ground.

You decide.

So every day you should be taking strategic steps toward your Ideal Business - steps that you've used this simple process to map out.

And if something isn't one of those steps and it's not fundamental to running the day to day of your business…when it comes to your professional life its WAY down the list of what deserves your attention.

And to give you a bit of perspective…for me, there are about 5 important tasks like that which I set out to accomplish each week.

Yes…weekly. Not daily.

If I can get 48 weeks of 5 significant tasks moving me toward my Ideal Business done…that's 240 over the year…I'll be just fine. And you will too.

So, stop being plagued by the disease of Self-Inflicted Overwhelm and start investing your time in building your Ideal Business.

Your Success Plan Made Simple

While I'd love to coach you to success – I'm going to give you the very simple planning process that I personally use…with no sales pitch attached and all right here so you can go through in just a few short minutes.

The Simple Success Planning System

The first thing that we all need to accept is that we're all busy…but usually we're busy just doing the things needed to get through the day rather than the things that will move us toward our Ideal Business as quickly as we'd like.

To avoid that, we need to plan how to move things forward in a simple process that actually has real world benefit.

So what each of us is going to do is set aside about an hour (no more than 90 minutes) for developing our business growth plan and the strategy we're going to use to make it happen.

Pull out a single sheet of paper, we're each going to answer these 3 questions:

1. Where do you want to go?
2. Where are you now?
3. How will you get from here to there?

Once we answer those questions we're equipped with everything we each need to take our businesses to the next level.

Question One: Where do you want to go?

For me this encompasses my Vision…what I want to be known for…and my Yearly Objectives…how I will measure success.

Here are 4 simple questions to help you figure out your Vision:

1. How good do you want to be?
2. What are you providing?
3. Who do you serve?
4. What is the geographic scope of your business?

My Vision is to be the World's #1 Solution for Helping Fitness Entrepreneurs to Build Their Ideal Businesses.

Objectives are measures of your success and your business performance.

To list your objectives:

1. Determine what you will measure. Keep it simple and straightforward.
2. Decide how you will measure it.
3. Describe specifically what the target is for each measure.

My Yearly Objectives aren't quite done yet, but here are a few that are still in the draft stage:

1000 Members in Virtual Fitness Mastermind

Increase Avg. Monthly Revenue by 25% While Maintaining Current Profit Margin

Increase Newsletter Subscriber Base By 33%

I'm still working through a few others for the year – but I'm close.

Question Two: Where are you now?

Once we've figured out where we want to go we need to get clear about where we are today and what has to change for us to get to where we aspire to be.

For each of us there are probably a bunch of little things standing between us and our Ideal Businesses – but for the purposes of planning we're going to focus on the 20% that will give us the 80% of the results we're looking for.

So in your business:

What has to change in your Marketing to hit your goals?
What has to change in your Selling to hit your goals?
What has to change in your Personnel to hit your goals?
What has to change in the Experience you provide to hit your goals?
What has to change in the Training you deliver to hit your goals?
What has to change in your Business Management & Finances to hit your goals?
What has to change in YOU to hit your goals?

Now, once you've written down those things that need to change, go through and rank them in order of importance. Then, starting at the top of the list - start thinking about what strategy would directly address and resolve that issue for you.

Keep that strategy list handy because you'll need it soon.

I'm still working through these myself right now...but here are some notes I've already jotted down:

Not enough consistency with paid traffic.
Not enough paths of entry to VFM.
Not enough Content Marketing.
Not enough 'Non-Course' Products.
My 'Division 3' is not developed enough.
Not 'sharp enough' at video, speaking.

Question Three: How will you get from here to there?

This is where we develop our Action Plan…a combination of our Strategies and our Priorities. Our Strategies are crucial because they give us the focus and clarity we need to set our Priorities by serving as the bridge from where we are to where we want to be.

Here's a simple way to get clear on your Strategies:

Desired Outcome [by] Strategic Decisions / Actions

Here's an example:

Increase Referrals [by] Implementing 3 Evergreen Referral Programs

Or…

Improve Coaching We Deliver [by] Providing Better In-House Staff Development

Once we've decided on our strategies, all that remains is to set priorities – to decide which Specific Actions we'll take and when we'll take them by. Now, the trick is to focus on the action and ideally the completion of the task or project by a specific date.

Here are a few examples of Priorities:

Launch a Point-of-Sale Referral Campaign by February 1st.
Complete a Public Speaking Course by May 1st.
Have a Paid Traffic Plan in Place that yields 50 Opt-Ins per Week by March 1st.

I try to limit the number of Priorities to about 5 per Quarter as we only 'get paid for done.'

And with that we're done.

The real strength of this sort of approach is that it makes your business growth plan come to life.

A good way to keep the plan current is to follow this kind of pattern:

Sometime this week complete the planning approach I just listed...then every 12 weeks or so, review and reset priorities...and celebrate progress.

And that's your Simple Success Planning System.

Nothing too complicated – but it's really effective. And if you're using our Ideal Business Game plan approach (the overall planning system we use to create our Ideal Businesses) – then this is a great yearly update.

So now, go put this into action.

Your Marketing Calendar

A couple of weeks ago I sent out an outline of what I'd do if I were running an adult fat loss or transformation type of business and it was very well received so I wanted to share it again.

Here's the overview and then a quick calendar below.

Overview

I'd start by applying the Interval approach that I developed where you essentially alternate sprints (high effort) with a more evergreen approach (lower effort).

I'd use the high effort periods to run my Transformation Contest type of promotions and really work to drive people into those - essentially pulling out all stops since they combine a deadline to register, and pretty specific in a defined time frame...that's about as good of an offer as you can have.

For those, I'd start about 4 weeks out and really do everything I could...at minimum:

FB Ads
Internal Signage
Mentions in sessions and an incentive to refer
A strong email promotion to my newsletter list
Press Release
Promotions on my Private FB Group

Then I'd mix in my evergreen stuff, which would essentially be a combination of list building and relationship marketing.

For the list building efforts, I'd develop two Lead Magnets, one encompassing a broad interest (like a healthy recipe guide) and one that would be more specific to my business (like a video series about the 5 Secrets to Achieving Your Own Transformation).

Then I'd drive traffic to those with FB Ads, find a few Strategic Alliance Partners to send out the recipe guide to their list and also get my current clients and newsletter subscribers to share them with their friends.

I'd set up a follow-up campaign (emails and calls) to get opt ins to come in for a Success Session.

For relationship marketing I'd have:

A point of sale referral promotion in place, something simple like: give me the names and emails of 3 friends and we'll invite them into a program as the new client's guest and give them the recipe guide as a gift.

I'd alternate a Bring-A-Friend Month with a Charity Workout - each promoted to get clients to bring guests. I'd invite my newsletter list to the Charity Workout.

Once a year I'd run a referral contest.

Twice a year I'd run a reactivation campaign.

I'd set up a Private FB Group and use it the way that we might have used a Fan page a couple of years ago before FB stopped showing posts to most of the people on the page.

I'd spend time each week networking and working on relationships with local business owners.

I'd send a weekly email newsletter.

It seems like a lot, but let me lay it out in a calendar:

January
Transformation Contest - pull out all the stops.
Reactivation Campaign (Promote Contest).
Bring-a-Friend the week before the Contest launches.

February
Charity Workout

March
Transformation Contest - pull out all the stops.
Bring-a-Friend the week before the Contest launches.

April
Charity Workout

May
Bring-A-Friend

June
Charity Workout

July
Bring-A-Friend

August
Charity Workout

September
Referral Contest (lead to TC)
Reactivation Campaign (lead to TC)
Transformation Challenge

October
Bring-A-Friend

November
Short Challenge leading up to Holidays
Charity Workout

December
Charity Workout

During each month I'd be doing the following:

Sending a weekly newsletter
Posting 1-3X per day in my private FB group
Running ads to my lead magnets and/or directly to free Success
Sessions
Networking
POS Referral Request for all new clients

This should take 5-6 hours per week if you're doing it well.

I'd set a goal of getting at least 150 new opt ins per month to start, but scale it up from there as my skill and budget grew - and I'd make sure my follow up was dialed in enough that I'd get an average of 25 prospective clients to walk in the door each month.

So there you have it...what I'd do if I were marketing your business.

You have ongoing relationship with marketing throughout the year and a few BIG events to drive people to…presumably your Transformation Challenges.

So now it's up to you.

You have a plan.

Go execute it!

The Rule of 3

By now you probably know that I like things 'simple.'

I like to explain things is a way that makes it easy for you to grasp too.

So one 'simple' thing that I do to help grow my business...something that I'm going to recommend to you as well...is to employ The Rule of 3.

Basically, each day I start with a To Do List like most anyone else, but I also identify the 3 Things That Would Make Today A Success.

If I only get 3 items on that list done - ideally those would be the 3.

Yesterday, I started with my list - which I'd written out the night before as usual. It was longer than most days because I'm traveling to a conference today.

I then identified my Big 3.

Well, sometime around 7:30 a.m. I got hit with a very unpleasant stomach 'bug' and most of the rest of my day was thrown off.

But I did get 2 of my 3 done.

(The one I didn't was reaching out to my new Online Fitness Entrepreneurs and Online Entrepreneurs Mastermind Groups.)

So in spite of feeling pretty awful, I still was able to get 2 important tasks to move my business forward done (and I probably only worked for about 45 minutes to complete those two.)

I'm not sure that most people can say the same in spite of working a full day.

That's the power of The Rule of 3.

So if you're using it - great. I'm sure you're seeing success.

If you're not - start. Today. You'll be glad you did.

5 Questions

I think that it's good to put your actions under the microscope. You need to see if you're moving closer to your goals…if not every day, at least every week.

Here are 5 Questions you can use to see how you're doing:

1. What new business did you generate this week?
2. What new prospects did you generate this week?
3. How did you nurture the relationships you have with your network?
4. How, specifically, did you move closer to your Ideal Business?
5. What did you do to improve your knowledge or skill set?

These are actually the questions Holly and I used to share what is going on in our businesses with one another when we meet.

This allows us to focus on both the present Production (Questions 1 & 2) and the long-term movement toward the businesses we want (Questions 3, 4 & 5).

The 5 Questions force you to think about selling and marketing each week, but also give you the balanced perspective of looking at things like retention (Question 3) or developing systems or checklists (Question 4) and keep the concept of continuing to learn and improve at the forefront (Questions 4 & 5).

If all you did was take 10 minutes on Saturday or Sunday to reflect on the previous week by running through these 5 Questions you'd almost certainly start becoming more productive and more focused on the things you need to be doing to build your Ideal Business.

A Gift For You

Bonuses for Reading *The Fitness Entrepreneur's Handbook*

As my way of saying 'Thank You' for reading the *The Fitness Entrepreneur's Handbook*, I've put together a collection of powerful, valuable resources to help you build your Ideal Business. You can access this collection of Bonuses, including:

- The 15 Minute Ideal Business Planner
- Proven Sales Scripts & Tools
- Marketing & Referral Systems
- And Much, Much More!

You can access this collection of bonuses at:

PatRigsbyBonuses.com

Proven Resources For Building Your Ideal Business

You can get access to the highest level of real world marketing, sales & business building education, process and tools though my collection of Ideal Business building programs.

Whether you want to build a successful personal training business in your local market, position yourself as the leading sports performance business in your area, grow your own online training business or launch a successful info-marketing business – I've developed proven solutions that will help you build the business that you want.

Find out which solution is right for you at:

IdealBusinessPrograms.com

The Ideal Business Show

Subscribe and listen to the Ideal Business Show Podcast on Itunes!

Pat interviews and shares the stories of successful entrepreneurs and experts like Todd Durkin, Eric Cressey, Mike Robertson and John Berardi who have built successful, lifestyle friendly businesses to help you do the same.

Access the podcasts at:

TheIdealBusinessShow.com

About the Author

Father. Husband. Entrepreneur. Coach. Author.

I guess if I were going to sum it up in 5 words, those would be the five. But I'm going to share a little more in hopes that my journey can be of a little help to you in your own.

I'm a 44-year-old guy that has built his share of successes from the ground up…and more importantly, have a beautiful wife, two incredible boys and a business that allows me to spend most of my time with them along with family and friends.

In the past decade, I've built over a dozen businesses as a CEO and Co-Owner, with five becoming million dollar or multi-million dollar ventures. Two of those businesses, Athletic Revolution and Fitness Revolution, have been multiple time winners on the Entrepreneur Franchise 500 with each being the #1 franchise for its respective market. Another business, Fitness Consulting Group, was a multiple time honoree on the Inc. 5000, placing as high as #580 on the list of fastest growing businesses in the U.S. I've also been a Best-Selling Author 6 times over, presented in front of thousands of entrepreneurs and been featured in *Entrepreneur*, *Men's Health*, *USA Today* and on hundreds of other media outlets.

When it comes to sales, I've personally sold as many as 116 franchises in a single year and been the strategist and copywriter for over 10 million dollars in online sales from my own businesses and millions more in sales for my clients.

In the fitness industry alone, my coaching & consulting clients have been featured in places like *Men's Health*, *USA Today*, *Men's Fitness*, *Shape*, *Women's Health*, *Huffington Post* and on ABC, CBS, NBC and pretty much any other media outlet you can think of. In addition to that, they've built some of the most successful businesses and brands in every corner of the industry, from local business and supplement companies to online businesses, certification organizations and even became bestselling authors. In fact, many (if not most) of the experts providing business coaching in the fitness industry have been my clients, customers or franchisees.

And the best part of this? I've been able to do all of these things and more while working from home, coaching my kids in baseball and soccer and enjoying a type of entrepreneurial lifestyle I would have never thought possible just a few short years ago.

How I Got Here…

I grew up in Portsmouth, Ohio not really interested in being an Entrepreneur…no, I wanted to be a Major League Baseball Player.

As I grew up and recognized that making the Major Leagues wasn't in my future (though I did have one very inauspicious season playing professional baseball), I set my sights on coaching.

At the age of just 23, I became the youngest College Head Baseball Coach in the country at Shawnee State University. While this may sound mildly impressive, I pretty much got the job because the program was in shambles and there weren't many people interested in the position.

Over the next 6 years, I built this program into a nationally competitive one, setting dozens of records and even finishing 5th at the World Series in 2000.

All this would lead you to think that things were rosy, but they weren't. There was a great deal of friction between myself and an administrator that led to my resignation and a complete change of direction shortly before I turned 30.

At the time, I referred to it as an early mid-life crisis, but being unemployed briefly gave me some time to decide what I wanted to do professionally with the rest of my life. My first 'career' as a baseball coach was rewarding and taught me many of the lessons I use today, but working in a corporate, bureaucratic environment just wasn't for me.

I knew that I wanted to own my own business, but in spite of growing up working as a janitor in my dad's small auto repair business, I really didn't know the first thing about being an entrepreneur.

Within a month, I took a position as a general manager at a baseball and performance training facility and did some personal training in the mornings to try to make ends meet. I started to study business, sales and marketing…the beginnings of my professional education. The baseball facility was sold and I moved to a role running the personal training in one gym, then later for all of the Gold's Gyms in Kentucky.

Going Into Business…

My home base for this position was Lexington, KY. There, not only did I meet my lovely wife Holly, but I also met a future business partner as I moved away from being an employee to being an entrepreneur.

Soon after, we first opened a personal training business in Elizabethtown, KY, then a health club in Owensboro, KY. We didn't have any money to get these businesses off the ground and at age 33 I found myself along with my wife and my then 3-year-old stepson living in the basement of a home that we shared with two roommates.

Before long we started to have some real success (yes, even moving out of the basement), and looking to expand. We began sharing what had worked in our own businesses with other fitness entrepreneurs. After attending an industry event that focused on online businesses, we focused more of our expansion in that direction and shelved the idea of adding more of our own gyms.

Over the next few years, what started as a small personal training business grew to a network of businesses ranging from franchises and certification companies to info-marketing businesses and real estate.

These days I've found my true professional calling – coaching and consulting with entrepreneurs who want more clients, more profits and more freedom to enjoy life. I've personally been able to build my 'ideal business' that so much is written about and I've done it at a time in my life when I had a family, a mortgage and many of the responsibilities that hold people back from pursuing their entrepreneurial dreams.

So if you want to build your ideal business…regardless of where you're at today…this book will give you the blueprint to get you there.

Made in the USA
Middletown, DE
23 October 2018